BEING TRANSFORMED BY GOD
IN THE WORKPLACE

BEING TRANSFORMED BY GOD
IN THE WORKPLACE

CRAWFORD G. CLARK

XULON PRESS

Xulon Press
2301 Lucien Way #415
Maitland, FL 32751
407.339.4217
www.xulonpress.com

Unless otherwise indicated, Scripture quotations taken from the Holy Bible, New International Version (NIV). Copyright © 1973, 1978, 1984, 2011 by Biblica, Inc.™. Used by permission. All rights reserved.

Scripture quotations taken from the Amplified Bible (AMP). Copyright © 1954, 1958, 1962, 1964, 1965, 1987 by The Lockman Foundation. Used by permission. All rights reserved.

Printed in the United States of America.

ISBN-13: 978-1-54567-334-8

TABLE OF CONTENTS

ACKNOWLEDGMENTS

I LIKE TO THANK MY LORD AND SAVIOR JESUS CHRIST WHO GUIDED ME through out the entire writing process and would give me the words to write on several occasions as I lay in bed in the wee hours of the morning. Everything that I am, I owe to you.

I like to thank my wife Beverly who was my sounding board through all the years I worked for the Fairmount Park Commission and later the renamed Park and Recreation Department. I love you with all my heart.

I like to thank my friend Nancy Campbell who graciously agreed to be my editor and to also provide the introduction for this book. Thank you so much.

INTRODUCTION

THESE DAYS, WE SPEND MUCH OF OUR TIME TRYING TO "BALANCE" OUR "life" with our "work"; but what if we are looking at these concepts all wrong? What if we stopped looking at life and work as mutually exclusive concepts, as two separate things that need to be balanced against each other? To do this, to create a new paradigm that allows us to see these two parts of our existence as being in concert with each other, we need to go back to the beginning. We need to go back to the original work model that was given to Adam in the garden where work began…perhaps even beyond that to the work of creation and the Creator.

In this thoughtful book, Pastor Crawford Clark helps us take a closer look at what God intended when He gave Adam the work of caring for the Garden of Eden. In so doing, The Creator did not make any distinction between Adam's living and the work he was charged with doing, unlike many Christians today who have compartmentalized their faith as only belonging in one place. Pastor Clark takes us from the very first work model of the Creator Himself, in the persons of the Trinity, through Adam and his God-given responsibilities, right down to how we, in the 21st century currently see "work" and "life" in the context of our faith. Do we drop our faith in the parking lot outside of our place of employ-ment and then pick it up when we leave? Or is it intended to be our living, breathing partner as we journey through all the places of our lives? We all have lives to live and we all have work to do. Pastor Clark helps us to see that, as Christians, if we are to carry out the work that God has given us to do in expanding His kingdom here on earth, we must begin to see the workplace as another venue to portray Christ's love, even if we never speak a word about it out loud. And, in introducing the concept of living our lives in "margin" rather ""balance, Pastor Clark gives us a part of that new paradigm we need to consider – I won't tell you what that is…you've got to read the book to find out!

This book is an easy read, but a deep dive at the same time. The plain language invites you to keep reading. At the same time, topics like Pastor Clark's examination of the intra- and interper-sonal issues that are part of what individuals deal with in the work-place will invite you to contemplate more deeply. I am certain it will help you to see how allowing your faith to manifest itself in *all* the places of your life can create that "peace that passes all under-standing" for you and those around you.

Enjoy!

Chapter 1

WHERE DID WORK ORIGINATE?

HERE WE ARE AT THE BEGINNING OF A NEW YEAR AND THE ECONOMY IS quite strong. With a strong economy, many people are working. In fact, the current unemployment rate is 3.9%. That is amazing, considering that 10 years ago it was above 8%. When we consider the jobs that are currently available, I am struck by the fact that many are not filled because people are not interested in them. Even though some folks might be in need of employment, they refuse to take interest in having certain kinds of jobs. That, of course, is their prerogative.

There are millions and millions of people who live in this country who are in pursuit of what we know to be the "American Dream." It is the dream that draws many to come to the United States from other countries…the dream that will have immigrants travel great distances seeking to attain it…the dream that many outsiders of the United States believe will change their lives as well as their family members' lives. It is a dream that many are willing to risk their lives to attain despite the many challenges and obstacles that undoubtedly are in their path trying to reach it. America, the land of wealth and opportunity has been good for many who have traversed the painful obstacles that were spread out like mines on a battlefield. Yes, America is quite bountiful, affording opportunity after opportunity, especially over the last hundred years, to those who were successful in finishing the journey. Yes, it has been quite bountiful for those who desire to use their talents and gifts for the betterment of others and the society at large. Work itself, not the concept, is the major reason why these dreamers were able to scale the mountain that stood in front of the dream. Work is what has been the backbone in reaching that dream and has been the big factor that has shaped and conditioned us as Americans for pursuit of it as well. We even start the process of preparing our children for the pursuit of the dream early in life through the educational system, the education that will ultimately lead them to desire some kind of employment.

We all have experienced someone asking us as children, "What do you want to be when you grow up?" Many will continue to ask, and even suggest possibilities such as a doctor, a lawyer, a teacher, a police officer, an engineer, etc. If we were to say something that would be considered way out there, people would have very interesting reactions. Can you imagine saying, "I want to be a garbage man" or "I want to clean toilets off an airplane" or "I want to be a custodian"? How about, "I want to be a missionary" or "I want to be a bible translator or a bible teacher or preacher?" In many cases, to say the least, people will have a funny look when it comes to the jobs just mentioned because there is not much money associated with those jobs.

For many, work is the most important part of life because it provides a means through which we operate and sustain our lives.

It provides an opportunity for the exchange of money for our time in helping to manufacture a product or provide a service. Work plays a major role in establishing the fabric of our lives and those we do life with. Think about all the jobs from which one is able to choose. The range of employment choices is quite exhaustive. We encounter the people who work in the various available employment capacities every single day of our lives. I am able to take my car to an automobile mechanic to get it repaired. I go to the grocery store to buy food and have to stand in line where I encounter the cashier. While in the store I see individuals stocking the shelves as well as a person who helps me at the customer service counter. I can even purchase dinner in the deli section and do some banking after coming from the checkout lane. Why not get a cake at the bakery? Meanwhile, I ask the butcher to cut my meat like I want it. Look at all the jobs at one location. I call my accountant when it is time to have my taxes filed. I meet with my financial adviser to go over my portfolio once or twice a year. I call the phone company, the electric company or the water company to go over an issue with my bill. I have the carpet man come to the house to clean the carpet. I call the hotel to make reservations for a trip that we are planning to take. Since we will be gone for a week, I contact the post office to inform them that we need to stop mail delivery for the week. I do the same with the newspaper delivery. Later that afternoon, I take my son to the baseball game where we can see the Phillies play. As we walk from the parking lot where we encountered the parking attendant collecting the money, we now pass by a small entrepreneur selling water and pretzels. Then we see the musician playing his saxophone providing entertainment for the people walking by. We then approach the stadium where we then are searched by security before we proceed to the persons collecting - or scanning - the tickets. Once we are truly inside the stadium, there are the great number of food locations where we can purchase our favorite food. Then there are the stores where we encounter the sale persons who will help us with the souvenirs and team apparel that is being displayed for purchase. Then there are the guys who are selling sodas, hot dogs, beer, water ice and cotton candy that walk around the stadium. What service; you don't even have to leave your chair! How convenient! These entertainment venues make it extremely easy for you to spend money. So, look at all the numerous jobs that we encounter just going to the supermarket or attending a ballgame.

All around us we find jobs being performed by people who might not necessarily enjoy their form of work, but they do it in order to survive. Many of the jobs require a college education; some require post-college training or a post-graduate degree in order to be able to work in the person's chosen capacity. Such jobs that fit into these highly educated categories include doctors, lawyers, administrators, university professors, etc. There are also jobs that can be performed without having college degrees, but require hours of training or mentoring in specific areas. Jobs like a plumber, electrician, carpenter, etc., would fit into this category. However, in order to reach the maximum potential in these trade areas, one must be licensed. Then there are jobs that only require a minimum of an eighth-grade education, not even a high school diploma. Several government jobs fit into this category. If a person has a general knowledge of the area in which they are applying and if they are able to pass a test and go through an interview process, then they can get a pretty decent government job that will be steady and provide a pretty good, stable life. There are landscaping jobs, service industry jobs, driving jobs, and security jobs, data entry jobs, computer software jobs as well as jobs in which one can provide home care services.

There is one thing that, no matter what job you have, all have in common, and that is a personal or relational component. Think about the number of hours that one is in the workplace. When travel time is included in the hours that are calculated along with the time spent relating to the job itself, the time spent in the workplace and in the presence of co-workers can be quite extensive. For most, the range would be 10 to 12 hours per day. For entrepreneurs, it would be much greater, possibly approaching 18 to 20 hours per day. That means, we spend from one- to two-thirds of our lives in a work environment. If this is indeed the situation, we should have a desire to know what skills, as well as behaviors, we need to be developing in order to grow as a person. With all the time that is being spent in the workplace, there have to be other areas of our lives that are impacted for the good. Is there something more that can come from all this time spent away from what we know to be family? In essence, can we actually call the workplace a family? In some instances, there are some workplace environments that feel like a family to employees. However, most workers in America don't experience that kind of environment. Maybe the question that should be asked is not whether the workplace should have a feel of family, but whether there parts of my life that God wants to see developed while I am part of the particular work community in which I find myself. The workplace might not feel like family, but it is indeed a community of which you are a part.

The genesis of work starts, of course, with God Himself. When God began to think about what He was going to do, in essence, God was working. Think about the many jobs that require creativity. This creative ability is part of God's imprint that was placed in humankind from the very beginning of its existence. Designers, engineers, artists, and musicians are very creative people and have the ability to put down on paper what they have come up with in their minds. Those who write stories and developed cartoon characters or movie scripts have the same ability. Authors, journalists, radio and television hosts, all have an amazing ability to think and ask very detailed questions on a regular basis. Thinking is work. Using imagination is work. When God spoke creation into existence, it was God then bringing to life what He envisioned in His mind. This was God working which, in our modern thinking, would be referred to as planning.

Maybe we need to look at work differently now that we can see that it was part of what God was doing before anything came into existence. The Bible says that God was in the beginning (Gen 1:1). The beginning consisted of Him; actually, it was God the Father, The Word (Jesus), and the Holy Spirit. The reason why I bring up this theological element is so that we can understand that God was in a relationship with others. This relationship consisted of three persons who are known as the Trinity. Since we know that God consists of three persons, we now are able to see that there must have been harmony between the three persons who make up God. It is necessary to understand this relational component because then we are able to see that all three persons of the Godhead were involved in the creation process; they agreed to do things as a team. This is a participatory management style that we see operating before God even created the world we live in. We are able to witness the involvement of those persons (Godhead) who are equal and have the same attributes and qualities. When you see a participatory management style in the workplace, it is nothing new. It was already in existence with God. The three persons of the Trinity shared responsibilities in the work of creation as well as the responsibility of being involved with Their creation on a regular basis. God does not overpower Himself; He works in harmony with Himself. When we see God creating in Genesis 2, we are able to see that He begins another phase of His work. He goes from the design phase to actually making it happen. He now implements the plan that He had designed in His mind and heart. God did not need paper to write down His design like we do. He was able to clearly design and see how it would be as well as what it would look like in the future. God worked for six days and then rested on the seventh day.

After God created the man, He placed him in the garden where He directed the man to care for the garden. He also gave the man the responsibility of naming the animals whom God had also created prior to the formation of man. Knowing that God gave the responsibility of caring for the garden and naming the animals is an indication that God values work. It also shows that work is part of God's nature. God would not be creating humankind just to sit around and do nothing; He wanted His Image Bearers to reflect who He was through what they did on a regular basis. Not only through the attributes of displaying love, loyalty and leadership among themselves, but to reflect an aspect of what God was doing when He created them, which was the aspect of work. He wanted man to be able to use his time doing something that was enriching to him and his future family as well as to bring glory to his Creator, God. Glory would be experienced by God as humankind put into practice what they were designed to do.

We are able to see that God had given Adam the opportunity of manifesting part of what was in God through the responsibility of carrying out what God had given him to do, which was his work. Within this element of work, which came from God's directive of caring for the garden, is a development component within the character of the man. Within the man are other attributes that are placed in him by God, which are also part of God's image. Many of these other attributes that are given naturally in man can be demonstrated through the implementation or manifestation of his work. Adam was working in what was also His home. Interesting! He had a job working at home. Does this mean that he was an entrepreneur? I don't believe so. However, there are some principles that can be derived from this original design that God established with the first family. We can say that Adam had a home-based job.

The work environment that Adam was a part of was created by God. The work was essential for the existence of the man. The work that he was assigned to do came from the Creator and consisted of using the human components that God had given him. What are those components? They are those elements that are a part of our being: the psychological, emotional, social, relational, physical, and spiritual areas of life. All of these areas were being used by man in the garden and are the same areas that we are made of today. We will be looking at these areas at various times throughout our journey regarding the workplace, along with our development as a person in the workplace.

I picture Adam's home in the garden as being something like a tropical rain forest with lush green foliage all around. The leaves on each of the plants are large with sparkling soft droplets of water falling from those leaves. This effect being produced by the mist that surrounds the ground. The sun creates a rainbow effect around the leaves, stimulating the senses with a vast array of color. I picture a large canopy of trees whose fingers are reaching to the sky, providing shade throughout many areas of the garden. As I gaze up at the top of the trees, I see the branches swaying back and forth like a choir with hands raised praising the Lord. The sunlight is peaking through, creating streaks of light streaming down to the ground creating an appearance of silvery glistening, like ice cycles flowing from the trees. What an amazing place the "Garden of Eden" must have been - paradise that we can only imagine! Man was given the wonderful assignment of caring for the paradise in which God had placed him. Adam, God's Image Bearer, is now to care for this paradise in which he resides.

What do you think about when you hear that term "care for?" My immediate thought would be a person who cares for someone else. I then think of a nurse in a hospital or facility who cares for a patient. There are several things that the nurse needs to do with regards to the care of a patient. There is the medication that is to be administered, usually on a time schedule. The patient's vital signs are checked regularly. Some nurses help to change the patient's clothes and give them a bath. They help with some of the grooming needs of the patient and possibly comfort them from a counseling perspective. If they do not actively engage in some of the care activity, they are supervising someone who is doing it. The nurse has to be ready and available to respond to the patient when they ring the bell or buzzer. There is continual care of the person from the time the person is admitted to the hospital or care facility until they are released. One who is a caretaker in this capacity would need to maintain an attitude that shows a continual focus on meeting the needs of the patient. The same type of care would be needed with a loved one at home. The care of a family member or friend would involve the same type of attitude or demeanor. People who are caregivers are usually sensitive, gentle, merciful, kind, loving individuals who are relational and enjoy serving others.

Let's go back to Adam in the garden. He is to care for the garden which would involve characteristics such as gentleness, long suffering, patience, sensitivity, love, pleasure, wonder, enjoyment, desire, adoration, satisfaction, attachment, significance and contentment. It appears that God, in some way, was giving man a way of developing a skill set that would be needed when it came to relationships. Work creates an environment for humankind to grow in characteristics that are directly tied into God's image. God hasn't given work to humankind to have a way to make money as a primary purpose. Work has evolved in such a way that that component is now a major factor. In fact, there was no money to be made when work was first introduced to man. Man was created perfect in the image of God, but God was then using work as a way to manifest other aspects of God in man. What did "care for" mean in the context of a paradise that had everything?

As a city boy who attended W.B. Saul High School in Philadelphia, a vocational agriculture school, I was introduced to the field of agriculture. As a Penn State graduate in the field of agriculture with an emphasis in agronomy, and as a 30-year park employee for the City of Philadelphia, I believe that I can possibly provide a reasonable answer to the question of what Adam might have needed to do in regards to taking care of the garden. I also believe that I can speak with a little knowledge about his other job dealing with the field of animal husbandry.

As I ponder a garden that has everything in it pertaining to plant material, most likely the Garden of Eden was created in a mature state. The first thing that comes to mind is the maintenance, which would involve weed management. Weeding a garden is one of the most labor-intensive operations in the maintenance of a flower bed. Since plant material, whether weeds or plants, have different reproductive cycles, there will be some types of seeds that are present continually throughout the growing season. These seeds that are produced by these mature plants will attempt to establish themselves in available locations on the ground within the flower beds and gardens. These seeds will begin to germinate and produce seedlings and plants which are now considered to be out of place. These out-of-place plant materials are now referred to as weeds. So now you know the definition of a weed. It is plant material that is out of place. The garden would need to be weed-free in order to maintain its pleasurable appearance.

The second component of maintenance would most likely be the overgrowth of shrubs and trees. This overgrowth would need to be cut off in some way. The cutting away of this type plant material is known as pruning. Adam could have broken the branches off or created some kind of cutting tool with which to cut the plant material. When there is too much overgrowth, fruit on the tree or shrub will be minimized due to the energy of the plant being channeled toward the green foliage. Another area of maintenance is the removal of the fruit from the tree or shrub so that other fruit might continue to be produced. All of the aforementioned conditions and maintenance procedures are just for maintaining the garden. Remember the garden was watered by mist or dew that would lay across the ground during the morning hours. There was no rain in existence at that time. Adam didn't have to be concerned with drought conditions at that point because God was the one making sure that everything was being watered.

Another type of maintenance that comes to mind is the repair of areas of erosion. We know there is not erosion that would be occurring due to rain, but erosion due to the animals tramping over certain areas was quite possible. In this case, Adam would need to cultivate these areas and replace damaged plant material with other material. That means that he would have to take part of a plant, or literally an entire plant, and move it to the area of need. Another possible job would be the removal of tree debris and leaves from certain areas. Inevitably, there was also grass. I have no idea how Adam would have cut the grass. Maybe the goats and the sheep were used to maintain these areas. Hey, it is possible!

Adam was to tend not only the garden, but he also had oversight of the animals. He was responsible for naming the animals that the Lord brought to him. Think about all of the animals and insects in existence. Adam was given the creativity as well as the capacity to name the creatures God had created. Is it possible that Adam also aided in the birthing of some of the animals as well? At Saul High School, I worked in the barn part time. Every now and then a cow that had been artificially inseminated would give birth to a calf and I would come in to help with this process. Because the cow wasn't able to completely push the calf out, the farmer and I would assist by pulling the calf the rest of the way. Sometimes the farmer, Mr.

Rozeman, would have to reach through the vagina of the cow to grab hold of the calf's legs in order to pull it out. Sometimes, he would have to twist the calf around while still in the inside because his or her head wasn't aligned in the proper position to come out. What an experience for me at such a young age! As you can see, I never forgot it.

Calves are extremely awkward at birth, having big heads and long legs. In many cases, sheep are the same way with the births. However, the difference is that many sheep will have multiple lambs. So, it is quite possible that Adam aided in the births of certain animals such as cows, horses, sheep, etc. It is also possible that Adam could have been involved with the genetic purity with the breeding groups and care of the plant life. Adam possibly would have actively been engaged with preventing the animals from overgrazing as well as preventing soil damage that could be caused by them.

We are able to see the different types of jobs that Adam could have been performing. Is this not a great manifestation of God in Adam, with the capacity to work? We see different types of work even here with Adam. We see the physical labor through gardening, the mental thinking through the naming of the animals, the various planning strategies that he possibly came up with regarding the garden and the animals, and the implementation of those strategies.

God desired to be in relationship with Adam, His creation, but He desired him to have purpose through the assignment that God had given him. God's assignments through work evolved out of the personal design in which God has created us. We all are uniquely different with various talents and God-given abilities. What we do as work also comes out of how we are wired, which is known as our temperament. What we do as a profession not only should be flowing out of a desire within us, but a passion that is directly attached to our being. The same purpose that was part of what God desired from Adam in the garden is the same substance and purpose that God desires from us today.

The work experience for many isn't seen through the grid of faith. The culture, as well as the workplace, brings about fear and intimidation when it comes to living out faith in the workplace. However, what is supposed to take place in the workplace for the believer? How is faith integrated with work and how does this faith change our lives as well as the lives of others? Is it possible to think separately about work and our faith or are they inseparable? Our perspective of work should be established by what we see in the pages of Scripture. There, we are able to see that, although work is attached to our fabric, which is the image of God, it should not be what defines who we are. God did not provide work for human-kind as punishment, but as a way to provide purpose and to bring glory to Himself.

As we examine work from a 360-degree perspective, we will be able to see that work can help make and shape us into the image of God's son, Jesus. Jesus was working every day during the time of His ministry, but He also worked as a carpenter and most likely helped His earthly father, Joseph, until the time of Joseph's death. Work, if looked at from a godly perspective, can provide us not only an avenue to receive remuneration, but also a place where God can do things in our lives both intra-personally and inter-personally.

We know that marriage is a major way that God is able to transform our lives, as a couple rubs against each other in the most intimate relationship God created. However, the next place where God can use people in our lives for transformational purposes is our job. God develops us through the interaction with people, people of all types. If the challenge for us is to love people as we love ourselves, what better place outside of the home, other than the workplace. Where there is work, there are people, and where there are people, there are issues. It is within the realm of issues with people that opportunity is created in the workplace for us to grow in faith as well as live out our faith. We will be looking at these areas throughout our journey through the wonderful world of the workplace. The workplace then can be seen as a transformational center that isn't like the building where believers gather to sing and hear the Word in the environment of community. But it can be seen as a place where the believer engages the world, culture, and the enemy (Satan) in order to put into practice those principles that are being instilled at the worship center. It is a place where believers come face to face with all of the challenges to faith that they can encounter. In the world of work, Jesus can be displayed and spiritual formation in our personal lives can be realized. Jesus can come to the workplace through us. Let's see what He is able to do when He is in the workplace with us.

Chapter 2

SELF-AWARENESS IS ESSENTIAL

IF YOU WOULD ASK MOST PEOPLE TO DESCRIBE THEMSELVES, MANY undoubtedly would do an adequate job when answering. However, how deeply can they go in their description of themselves? Yes, it is possible to give surface descriptions, such as whether they are an introvert or extrovert, whether they love to be around people or not, what are their favorite type of clothes to wear or what types of food they like to eat. We might even be able to say what gives us energy or what we have a passion for regarding things we enjoy doing. These descriptions are adequate, but don't fully describe how we are designed by God. Understanding how we are designed by God on a personal level can help us know ourselves in a deeper way. In order to get a real look at who we are and what makes us tick, we have to be tested with one of the many tests that measures our temperament, or what many will call personality tests. A personality test is a questionnaire or a standardized instrument designed to reveal aspects of an individual's character or psychological makeup. The first personality tests were developed in the 1920s. There are several in existence today and many of these tests are available easily on the web. However, the more comprehensive tests are still the DISC or Myers Briggs. The Arno Profile System measures temperament, however, which is different than the personality tests.

Many places of employment these days will require their potential employees to take a test before they come to work for them. Some even require these tests as part of the hiring process. Why? The employer wants to know or have some idea about who the potential employee is as a person. They want to be able to know what their tendencies are when it comes to people and how they possibly will respond to the various daily situations that will be encountered. Also, there is a need, to some degree, to be able to determine the potential productivity that the employer will be able to get from the employee. Every employer, however, will not provide these kinds of tests themselves. These tests are available at any time online and can be taken by any person if they so desire. However, most individuals probably will not take one of these tests on their own, considering that there is a cost involved.

The workplace is not the only situation where these tests are administered. When I applied to go to Eastern Baptist Seminary several years ago (now Palmer Seminary), it was required that all potential students take the Myers Briggs. The Myers Briggs is a very comprehensive test that, at the time, was three hours in length; there is a shorter version available today. It measures in depth the characteristics that make up the person. The Myers Briggs instrument provides information to determine the needs in the area of relationships, evaluates the ways in which a person perceives the world, and helps them to understand how they make decisions. The test judges the person's preferences across four dichotomies, each of which is represented by a letter in the results: Introversion (I) Extroversion (E), Intuition (N) Sensing (S), Feeling (F) Thinking (T), Perception (P), Judging (J). It appears that it was necessary for the Seminary to give this test to students to determine psychological as well as social strengths and weaknesses. In other words, they wanted to know what the student's communication style would be, as well as their ability to adapt to other students and faculty and the overall school environment.

I recently talked to a friend of mine who is a dentist and has started a practice in Plymouth Meeting, Pennsylvania. He told me that he had his employees take the DISC test. He wants to have an office that promotes harmony among the employees, as well as have his staff interact with the patients well. If the employees are aware of their strengths and weaknesses, especially in the area of communication, they can then get some coaching, if necessary, and learn how to be able to handle themselves appropriately and to also identify the areas of need in their lives. Every person is not naturally a team player. In some of the tests that are administered, animals are used as descriptors for the characteristics associated with the person. For example, in one of the tests that I took with AACC (American Association of Christian Counselors), there were four animals that were used in the description. They were the lion, otter, golden retriever and beaver. The lion and beaver represented those individuals whose proclivity is to lean more toward the decisive, organized, get-things-done characteristics, while the otter and golden retriever leaned toward the relational, laid back, team player characteristics. There are individual variables that make each animal category separate, but I linked the ones that are in the same quadrant. When an employer is able to know how his or her people are wired, they can maximize not only the potential of productivity, but enhance the quality of the individuals' lives.

All the tests described here are merely tools that can help us become self-aware. Self-awareness is necessary to truly understand the best positions in which to place ourselves, as well as how to properly interact with others.

There is a great example in the Scripture that can help us delve into the area of self-awareness as well; it is found in I Kings Chapter 3. When Solomon became king, he was asked by God in a dream by night "What shall I give you." Solomon acknowledged about himself that he was a little child when it came to running a kingdom. He then went on to ask God for an understanding heart in order to judge God's people and to discern between good and evil. In other versions of the Bible, it is called wisdom. God then gave him what he asked for: "wisdom", along with some additional qualities and riches which he didn't request. In the same chapter, we see Solomon demonstrate this wisdom with two women who had come before him with an issue. The issue was in regards to who was the true mother of a child. One of the women had laid on her child while sleeping during the night and the child died. The woman who laid on the child then took the other mother's child as hers and placed her child with the other mother while she slept. When the mother whose child had been taken woke and saw that the child next to her was dead, she knew that the child wasn't hers. The other woman insisted that it was. This matter came before the king and he was able to use wisdom to determine the real mother. Think about what Solomon had just done. He was able to now see the result of what he had asked God to be able to do. Because he was self-aware and was able to recognize that he needed a quality far beyond what he had on his own to govern people, he asked God for what he knew he lacked.

Through Solomon, we are able to see the ability and advantages of knowing one's self. To have an accurate self-assessment of oneself as a person is a crucial element of navigating the waters of life. There are so many people who meander through life like a toy sail boat in a stream that heads out to the river. That toy sail boat is just floating along with no purpose or meaning. It is just there in the water moving along until it gets stuck on something or is carried to a bigger body of water to do the same thing, just float until it is removed somehow, either ending up on land or in the belly of a big fish! I am not trying to be funny, but rather illustrate how some people are just floating in life, merely existing, with no purpose. They live day to day going through a routine. They will continue to do what they do until they retire, changing the pattern slightly at that point possibly, and then continue to do what they do until they die. Life was meant to be more than meandering in a stream not knowing where you will end up. Life was meant to have purpose and direction and to bring glory to God. In a very big way, God uses the workplace to help provide the necessary lubrication as well as the calibration for the navigation system of our lives.

When a person is self-aware, they are living a life that is filled with truth. Maybe the tragic issue here for many people is that truth is hard to accept. How many people do you know love truth? The number appears to be getting slimmer and slimmer as the culture changes. Truth is becoming a lost commodity as the culture moves quickly away from the principles of God's Word to the philosophy of man. The interesting thing about those who are able to see truth is that they might have a problem seeing it in their own lives. Truth, when it is in regards to self, is hard to receive because we tend to believe that " I am not that bad." Those outside of us, however, are able to recognize characteristics or patterns in our lives that we cannot see. Individuals who point out such imperfections and flaws to us are doing us a great service and are being used by God to shape us through truth. Being able respond well to these truths about ourselves and to change through the input of others is part of the process of how we become self-aware. Self-awareness and truth go hand in hand and are both essential aspects of how God brings depth to our character.

I remember when I first became a District Manager in the Fairmount Park System. Part of my job as a manager was the handling of disciplinary issues. As a person who loves people and has the proclivity to want to be liked by everyone, handing out discipline was very difficult for me. However, I knew that it was part of the job. Shortly after being in this new position of responsibility, a situation arose with an employee who continued to ignore all of the verbal warnings I gave him. I was hoping that he would listen so that I would not have to resort to writing him up. However, he would not heed those verbal attempts to get him to alter the behavior, and it became necessary for me to use paper. As I proceeded to handle this disciplinary issue, I spoke to my superior about the matter. He said something to me that stuck with me the rest of my managerial career. He told me, "Crawford, you need to remember that you are not the one who is bringing the discipline down on the person; they are doing it to themselves. You are giving them what they asked for." I never forgot that statement.

When a person continues with a certain behavior that is against the company's standards or policies, the supervisor or person in charge is merely seeing to it that the policy is being enforced. When the person is refusing to adhere to the policy they are, in essence, asking the discipline to be given to them by not keeping that policy. If I were to allow the policy to be broken continuously by the employee, to a large degree, I would not be doing what I am being asked to do by the employer. Now, I have placed myself in the position of being not just like the employee that is violating policy, but I am also failing to keep policy from being followed. Consequences are necessary when employees fail to keep the policies of the employer or when they fail to adhere to the rules that have been established. Isn't God the same way? He brings about consequences in our lives when we fail to be obedient to Him.

Paul says in I Cor. 11:28 "A man ought to examine himself before he eats of the bread and drinks of the cup." This verse is within the context of Paul writing to the church at Corinth concerning their behavior during communion. They are exhibiting inappropriate behavior at the communion feast. Paul is addressing the issue by telling them to take an assessment of their heart and their motives prior to eating the bread and drinking the wine. Many of them were being judged by God and suffering consequences, some even death, because of their behavior. Taking an assessment of our lives or aspects of our lives should always be occurring, not just prior to receiving communion. The principle of self-examination should be a part of what we do in life as a normal and regular process. The input of others in our lives is also a part of our examining ourselves.

The earlier that we can understand that corrective criticism is a positive in our lives and that sometimes the way it is given to us might have to be ignored, the better we will be able to accept it. By the same token, we must realize that it still remains a great asset in our lives. Thousands, even millions, of people do not know how to receive criticism or handle it, especially if given to them incorrectly. Self-awareness will aid us, even when things are said inappropriately. How? If a person is very self-aware, that characteristic will provide an assessment grid by which they are able to process the information received. When the criticism is heard, the person can take from it what is necessary, but will be able to respond to the alleged offending person in a wise manner. As believers, we can't be moved by emotion and definitely cannot allow the emotion to interfere or get in the way of logic. The response must be one that has been filtered through the grid of wisdom. This ability can only come by way of our being changed by truth and by walking with the Holy Spirit. Growth can get us there, but surrender will *keep* us there.

There are several models in the Scriptures that can give us insight on how we can handle ourselves through being self-aware. Consider John the Baptist in John 1:19-32. As we examine the dialogue that was taking place between John the Baptist and the priests and Levites, we can see that John knows who he is and his place regarding his role in life. The priests and Levites asked him who he was: "Are you the Christ?" "Are you Elijah?" "Are you a prophet?" He then answers their question. He says, "I am the voice of one crying in the desert." This is an amazing answer! John then tells them that there is one that is among them who they do not know that is greater than he. He was referring to Jesus, of course. John says that he is a voice. A voice that is proclaiming what? He is proclaiming the Word, who is Jesus. John isn't Christ, but he is a spokesperson for Christ, preparing the way for Christ. John knows without any doubt who he is and what he is meant to do. He is able to handle himself appropriately as the priests and Levites were making him out to be somebody great. He actually could have received what they were saying and exercised pride, thinking he was this great person, he did not do that. He stayed in his position and understood that Jesus was the one who was to be the important one. He even made the statement that he is unworthy to untie His shoes. This is a great example of a person being self-aware.

There is a another example or model when it comes to self-awareness, That is Jesus Himself. The best example that I can see is when Jesus is in the desert being tempted by Satan. Matthew 4:1-11 shows the description of what occurred. We are able to see Jesus in His humanity, as being subjected to temptation of His flesh during a fast. Can you imagine not eating for forty days and, while in the middle of it, being subjected to the constant barrage of those pressuring you to give in and eat? Jesus was being pressured by Satan to provide His own food if He was hungry, and Jesus was indeed hungry. We know that Jesus is God; however, He has surrendered His power and is being led by the Spirit at this juncture. He is feeling in His body and mind everything that we would feel in ours. He is also being challenged emotionally and psychologically when Satan asks Him to do the three things that Jesus is able to do but refuses. What was at the heart of Satan challenging Jesus to tell the stones to become bread, throw himself off the highest point of the temple, and to bow down and worship him (Satan), was to get Jesus to sin. If Jesus would have sinned, He would not have been able to be our Savior. Satan was attempting to get Jesus not to be aware of who He was and to have self-doubt, like he did with Eve, and then Adam, in the garden. Satan wanted Jesus to acknowledge him by being obedient to his words, instructions, and requests. Self-awareness on Jesus' part kept Him from yielding to the temptation of Satan. Self-awareness in the midst of weakness protected Him from making a decision that He would regret. It kept Him in His purpose. Self-awareness provided an avenue of remaining steadfast to the Father. It enabled Him to identify what were lies and deception. Self-awareness kept Him in the will of the Father. It would eventually provide an example for those who would follow Him.

The difference between us and Jesus in regards to self-awareness is that ours must be developed through community and through personal surrender to the Holy Spirit. We are being developed from a fallen state or sinful condition. It is through God's Spirit of truth by which we are guided in truth as we are open to it. God uses community, whether Christian or non-Christian, to provide critical and necessary information that will impact our lives over time. The workplace is a huge community that God uses to not only challenge our self-awareness while we are there, but to mold our self-awareness while we are there.

In 2 Samuel 11 we are able to see the story of David and Bathsheba. You can read the story for yourself to get the background. In chapter 12 we see Nathan the prophet come to David to inform him of what he (David) has done. So that you will know what is going on, I will give a little bit of information. David has committed adultery, had the husband of the woman with whom he committed adultery killed, and then takes the husband's wife to be his wife. This is a modern day R-rated movie. This story could possibly qualify for at least a Golden Globe! Now that I have given you the juicy stuff, let's get to the point I would like to make. David has sinned against God and has exhibited and carried out behaviors as a king that have grieved the heart of God. Notice in Chapter 12 that God's prophet was instructed by God to go to King David at his job to give him a message.

David is king, which is a job. We might not look at the monarchy that way, but it is indeed a place of employment in which the king rules and is responsible for millions of people. All of the nation's firstborn males were required to enter into service of the king. We can find reference to this in I Samuel 8. David had lost his sense of self-awareness due to the sin he had committed and was still living in it. One of the consequences of unconfessed sin is the insensitivity to sin and the inability of hearing and listening to the Holy Spirit. God, because of His love toward David sends the prophet into his life to give a word from God. This word was direct and poignant to his unconfessed sin that placed him in a backslidden condition (out of fellowship with God). When David acknowledged his sin, he confessed to God. We are able to benefit from David's sin and his subsequent repentance through his penning of Psalm 32 and Psalm 51. David's experience of going through a time of not being self-aware provides us with great insight that will help us to be self-aware.

It is essential that we become self-aware in our lives. This quality will benefit us in so many ways and will also protect us in ways that we never thought possible. Knowing who we are will provide a framework to establish proper relationships in our lives, as well as to help set proper boundaries in our lives. Just think about how we can avoid many troubling issues that, almost always, are self-inflicted and how we will be able to properly address people when they talk to us in many inappropriate ways. Talk about a transformed life! It starts with knowing ourselves from an honest perspective and remaining in a mindset that helps us to be self-aware.

Chapter 3

THE NEED TO UNDERSTAND PEOPLE

IF THERE WERE EVER AN AREA IN LIFE IN WHICH MANY PEOPLE DO NOT gain a skill, it is the area of understanding people. It appears that most don't see the need to acquire such a vital and necessary skill. Many don't believe that it is necessary to understand others. Yet it is one of the most important elements that can be placed in your arsenal of personal development. Many feel that as long as they can get their own point across to others, no matter how rudely, that is all they need to be able to do in life. This is the mindset of many intelligent people and their concern for others seems to be at a minimum, especially in the workplace.

Diversity of people groups in the workplace these days has made it even more difficult to understand those who are there. If a husband doesn't take the time to understand his wife or the teacher doesn't take the time to understand her or his student – or if the pastor doesn't take the time to understand his or her congregants or an employer doesn't take the time to understand his or her employees - then how is personal growth and personal satisfaction with all parties going to be realized? There has to be more involved with work than just deadlines, quotas, meetings, paperwork and productivity. There has to be interaction among the workers. This interaction, in many cases, will center around responsibility, trust, respect, humility and integrity. But without a clear understanding of our loved ones or people in general, and knowing what they truly are in need of, how will we be able to enhance or increase their value in life? As for the workplace, without being able to connect well, how are we able to serve well in any capacity?

When it comes to people, inevitably we can find many types. What do I mean when I use the term "type?" I am talking about people with different personalities and temperaments. I am talking about how individuals interact with the world on all levels, how they interact with people, places and things. Each individual is different and will relate to the world in a different way. These ways, some of them peculiar, will be witnessed and experienced in the workplace by co-workers. So the question becomes, "How do we respond to these behaviors that we undoubtedly will inter-face with?"

There are many variables that go into the make-up of a particular individual. We know that chromosomal make-up is part of what plays into who a person ultimately becomes. However, learned behavior is also a major factor that plays into how the person develops. One factor that is often overlooked, especially by people without a spiritual belief system, is a person's faith. Specifically, those who come to know Jesus, in many ways, are misunderstood. Some believers occasionally exhibit some peculiar behavior that is derived from their misinterpretation of Scripture or their ignorance of how to practically and correctly incorporate biblical principles into their lives. Jesus, when He is truly Lord of a person's life, changes their life in a magnanimous way. This change that is experienced by the person impacts their entire life and dramatically affects their behavior. Out of all the experiences that a person can have in life, the only experience that is transformational for everyone is the cross of Christ. At the foot of the cross, every person is on the same playing field no matter what background, ethnic group, pedigree, or class. Cancer is a life-changing event; the death of a child is life-changing; living through war is life-changing. But that kind of life-changing can make a person bitter, withdrawn, angry, sullen or pessimistic. The cross of Christ is different; it is more life-transforming or transmuting in such a way that lifts the person up toward a deeper relationship with God each and every time, not pulling them downward into negative or detrimental behavior.

Consider the other variables that come into play that will have impact on how individuals are molded and shaped. We are clearly able to see that cultural norms within a society will help to shape the thinking of those in that culture. Whether a person is Egyptian, Korean, African, African American, Chinese, Middle Eastern, German or Russian or any other nationality, their ethnic background will be part of who they are and possibly what they become in life. Traditions, rituals, ways of thinking, as well as other aspects of their culture will impact their lives and, most likely, those individuals who are close to them as well. If there happens to be multiple ethnic groups in the family, then there will be a blending of the cultures that make up that family. As multiple generations are formed out of that family, personal choice of what cultural traditions to bring forward into the new family structure will be determined by each individual that came from this blended cultural home.

In addition to the cultural fabric, birth order is to be considered. Depending on where one is in the family birth order, specific behaviors may be exhibited by a person due to that position. There is scientific evidence that birth order impacts the behavior of children These behaviors can be quite apparent when observed and are very evident in the family structure and dynamic. Many of these behaviors will remain with a person for their entire life and will also manifest in the workplace. A great book to read on birth order is " The Birth Order Book" by Dr. Kevin Leman. It is based on over 30 years of extensive research in the field.

Looking at this issue from the perspective of Scripture, we are able to see significance in the behaviors of the Jews, Gentiles, and Samaritans. It is quite apparent that what we see in their day is the presence of what we would call in our world today, sexism, racism and classism. I don't know about you, but I appreciate the fact that God included plenty of examples in His Word centered around the bad behavior of people as a group, especially the impact on culture. We are able to see these behaviors over a period of two thousand years with different generations. With this understanding from a Biblical perspective, we are able to see that it doesn't matter what period of time or generation; people are alike when it comes to how they behave. When we see Jesus interacting with people during the time that He was ministering on earth, we see that He walked right into the traditions and prejudices that had plagued humanity since the fall of humankind into sin. The behaviors that were being exhibited by humankind - sexism, racism and class-ism that would be confronted by Jesus - were all rooted in sin that was deeply embedded in the heart of humankind. Jesus had come to change humankind's predicament through his finished work on the cross.

The Jews were the people that God choose to use in order to represent Him before the nations. This act of choice by God was out of sovereignty. In other words, He did it because He wanted to do it. Throughout the entire Old Testament, at least from the time of Moses, we see a system of worship that really did not allow people to get close to God. How do we know that? We know because we see God setting Himself apart from the people in worship through the veil that was in the Temple. This veil served as a barrier and symbolized the separation between God and humankind. God even sets Himself apart from the priests. Only the High Priest could enter into the Holy of Holies once a year for the atonement of the people's sin. The Jews began to get prideful and to put a strangle hold on the people by creating rules on top of rules that the people were required to follow. These requirements, implemented by the Jewish leaders (Pharisees, Sadducees, Scribes, Priests, Levites,) made it extremely difficult for the Jewish people. These same rules were also applied to Gentiles who would become Jewish. Gentiles were considered sinners, not worthy of what God had given to the Jews. The Gentiles, however, could become Jewish if they believed in Yahweh and would follow the rules of life that were established by the leadership. For example, in order to become Jewish, circumcision was required.

The Samaritans - half breeds of the Jews - were despised and hated by the Jews. In fact, the Jews didn't associate with Samaritans or talk to them. Can you see the parallel here with our society today? There are those in our modern day who hate and despise other groups of people. They only go so far when it comes to having personal relationships with certain people or ethnic groups, if they do it at all. The ancient world that Jesus stepped into was dealing with the same issues that we deal with today. People, no matter where they come from or what their nationality might be, are cut from the same cloth. We then see Jesus, who is in the lineage of the Jews, intentionally crossing over cultural and ethnic barriers in order to have relationship with a person with whom He is "forbidden" to interact as a Jew. Jesus understands the cultures, traditions, backgrounds of all the people with whom He had dealings, as well as the attitudes of those who were mostly responsible for the prejudice - that is, the church's leadership.

What are we able to see with the example of Jesus and His interaction with those who were against Him is that He understood them. It didn't matter if they understood Him or not. He knew that their attitudes and behaviors were not pleasing to the Father. No matter what they thought about Him or how they felt toward Him, He had to stand for righteousness and *be* the truth for those who thought they were giving truth. He was able to cross the lines of separation (see John 4) and give a person what they were in need of: life and change – a permanent change. Part of understanding people is knowing some of their background, which means having an awareness of a person's ethnicity and some of the differences that are between them and ourselves. We also need to know how seriously the person believes in their own cultural and ethnic norms. So how do we attain this insight?

There are two primary ways that I believe we can get insight in the area of a person's culture. First, we must be students and learn those things that we do not know about another person's culture. Second, we must communicate with the person that is different from us and take an interest in them. They can provide a tremendous amount of information about themselves if we ask the right questions and let them speak. We genuinely should have a strong interest in them. As we seek to do this with individuals, we are gaining valuable insight that can be used both in the present and the future. The more we learn regarding groups of people, the more we are growing in our understanding of people in general. Jesus, though He was God, lived out of the limelight until age 30 when He started His public ministry. What do you think He was doing during these quiet years that are not mentioned in Scripture? I believe that He was living a life like any other person during that time. He was being educated, living among ordinary people and developing relationships with family, neighbors, friends and co-workers.

Paul also demonstrated the value of understanding people from a cultural perspective. He was born a Jew, studied and rose in ranks to be a Pharisee that was in the Sanhedrin (church leader in the body of the Synagogue). He was a Roman citizen, which gave him the flexibility to move in Roman-occupied cities freely. He also was schooled in Greek culture and language. He was able to speak in Hebrew, Greek and Aramaic. Paul was extremely smart and understood both the people and the cultures of his day. Through this understanding, he was able to minister the gospel in specific ways to each of these groups of people. In fact, he went on three missionary journeys encompassing several cities in the ancient world. Paul was able to relate to the people in all of these locations which led to him becoming the preacher to the Gentiles. However, the Jews were continuously rejecting the message that he was preaching.

One of the important things that I hope you are able to see is that having a reservoir of understanding regarding people's backgrounds in general will aid in our understanding of individuals.

Another key factor in understanding people is to identify what generation the person is a part. Take a look at the following chart:

	Start of birth	End of Birth
The Greatest Generation	1910	1924
The Silent Generation	1925	1945
Baby Boomer	1946	1964
Generation X (Baby Buster)	1965	1979
Xennials	1975	1985
Millennials (Generation Y)	1980	1994
1 Gen/ Gen Z	1995	2012
Gen Alpha	2013	2025

Source (https://www.adducation.info/lifestyle/generation-names/)

Seven of the eight generations mentioned above are encountered on a regular basis by most people. Four of the eight we will most likely encounter in the workplace, unless it is a home-based or small business. There are a particular set of characteristics that are generally indicative of those who are part of any of these generations. There are exceptions, of course but, in most cases, the exceptions are due to changes in the person's life that are brought about due to beliefs or incidents that have altered their behaviors.

The question might be asked, "Why is it necessary to understand generations?" The reason is that thinking patterns, societal norms, approaches to problem solving, perspectives on life, are generational in nature. In order to connect with individuals outside of one's own family that are from different generations, we need to be familiar with these types of differences. What was taught in school and how it was taught is different among generations. Technology and the use of technology is different. The use of technology impacts learning and has had a major impact on how information is accessed as well as the speed in which it is accessed. When you consider individuals who are a decade apart in age, in order for them to connect with each other on some level, they have to be familiar with the differences among their generations, even though they have some similarities. Relationships are established through connection. The necessary piece in workplace relationships might be the desire to connect with those individuals who we do not understand or are quite different from us.

Just think why it was so difficult for many people during Jesus' time to receive what He had to say. He claimed to be from heaven and that His Father was God. Imagine how that sounded if one just heard it for the first time. It takes faith to accept such a claim. The element that made the difference for many of the Jews was the signs that Jesus showed through the miracles that He performed. No one could do the things that He displayed: healing the sick, changing water into wine, casting out demons, raising people from the dead, causing the blind to see, enabling the cripple to walk, and so forth. The greatest of all these signs, of course, was forgiving a person of their sin. He was indeed God because only God could do such things that were obviously major displays of power. It took faith to accept Jesus, and it still takes faith today to believe that He is who He says He is - the Savior of the world. These signs, which demonstrated the creative power that only God possesses, were part of the same power that created the earth and everything in it, including humankind.

We see Jesus, the One from heaven, the One who created and knows everything about everybody, is attempting to bring truth into the cultural, generational, and traditional establishment that segregates people and produces an environment of prejudice and separation. Aren't we being like the Scribes and Pharisees when we stay separated from each other, whether in our neighborhood or in the workplace? People today want to be isolated, which isn't what God desired or how things were meant to be, especially not the way in which we were created. God desires relationship and the enhancement of relationships through having Him in the midst of them. When we are able to understand people through intentionally stepping into their world, we find that we are able to get access into areas we never thought possible. We are able to speak into situations only because we have taken the time to know that person and God gives us the ability at times to see into the person's soul in order that we might be able to be used to bring healing and change. That is how God wants to use the people of God in the workplace, when appropriate.

We have examined briefly the generational perspectives as well as the cultural aspects that undoubtedly have an effect on individuals. As we begin to look at people as individuals, we now begin to see them from an eyewitness view. The person in front of us is who we encounter on a regular - or somewhat regular - basis. When we interact with that person, we will encounter various characteristics that make that person who they are. Inevitably, there might be some characteristics that the person may possess that rub us the wrong way. The question is, how should we respond? We tend to react to situations and circumstances instead of *responding* to them. Responding to those circumstances gives us time to think before we move or talk or exhibit any action. Reacting to circumstances is immediate and usually is accompanied with emotion and impetuous action(s) or thought(s). It is in this arena that God wants to change us and allow us to help others in the way we interact with the characteristics of people, especially the individuals with whom we have difficulty. The key is to understand them. But *how* do we actually accomplish that?

When you attempt to get your children to listen to you, what do you do? You talk to them several times, grab them to get their attention, yell at them, etc. Some of these tactics may work, but in many cases, they won't. We want our children to listen to what we say because the information we want them to have, we believe, will help them. Did you catch that? Let me say that again: We believe that the information we want them to have will help them. When it comes to our children, we want to help them. We are part of their development and we attempt to impart prudent instruction to them so that they will develop and have a skill set when it comes to inter-personal relationships. We call this process with our children parenting. So, in our relationships at work, what should our thinking be? Yes, we are there to do a job or perform a task, whether producing a product or offering a service. On a human level, however, what can we bring to the people in the workplace and what should we be getting from them in the workplace. As we engage with the people in the workplace, how are we impacted on a deeper level within our being?

There has to be a greater purpose that accompanies our work experience that goes beyond just work itself, and that is the addition of value to fellow human beings as one works alongside them. That concept or way of thinking should be part of the mindset of a believer in the workplace. This concept evolves out of the statement that Jesus gives in Matthew 5:13-16.

> **13 "Let me tell you why you are here. You're here to be salt-seasoning that brings out the God-flavors of this earth. If you lose your saltiness, how will people taste godliness? You've lost your usefulness and will end up in the garbage.**

> **14-16 "Here's another way to put it: You're here to be light, bringing out the God-colors in the world. God is not a secret to be kept. We're going public with this, as public as a city on a hill. If I make you light-bearers, you don't think I'm going to hide you under a bucket, do you? I'm putting you on a light stand. Now that I've put you there on a hilltop, on a light stand—shine! Keep open house; be generous with your lives. By opening up to others, you'll prompt people to open up with God, this generous Father in heaven.**

Salt enhances the flavor of food as well as serves as a preservative for meat. How do we enhance the "flavor" of people's lives at work through our engagement with them? How am I changed by their interaction with me, whether it is a negative or a positive experience? What are the characteristics of light? Light shines into darkness. We need to ask ourselves this question, "In the workplace, where there can be a lot of darkness, how is my light - if I have one - having an impact on their darkness?" A light exposes the things that are hidden when in darkness. Am I able to be in a posture where the light can go in both directions? The light that evolves from me shines in the life of others and the light that evolves from others as well as the darkness from others can expose the lack of light that might be missing from my life. God can expose our lack of light through the darkness of others. I find that to be quite intriguing. We have areas in our lives that are impacted by the darkness of others which, in turn, exposes our own areas that are in darkness. This happens because the Holy Spirit, who lives in the believer, is able to shed light when the darkness is exposed. Their darkness prompts the exposure of our darkness, where there should be light.

Our lives are to provide salt and light no matter where we are. Our lives are to enhance the lives of those we encounter, and to shine a light so that the love of Christ can be experienced. This mandate does not stop when we go to work. So how can we accomplish this feat? It starts first with understanding people. As we talk about the other topics within the book, the underlying theme of understanding self and others will be interwoven throughout the pages. If you don't remember anything else from this chapter, remember this: The key to understanding people is to seek to understand them even if they don't understand you.

Chapter 4

THE DYNAMIC OF IMMATURITY

AS A SEVEN YEAR OLD BOY, YOU ARE NOT THINKING ABOUT WHETHER YOUR actions or behaviors are immature. You are just doing whatever enters your mind at the time. Most children at age seven would not be thinking about how what they are doing is having an impact on others. Most children cannot even rap their heads around the concept of maturity, but yet there are adults who expect their children to be mature even though the adults might not be.

I recall an incident that happened while on vacation with my aunt in my early years. It occurred at the age of seven to be exact. While traveling on a Greyhound bus through various states across the country, we had to have layovers of a few hours on several occasions. I remember, while in the bus station in Cheyenne Wyoming, I was turning somersaults in the middle of the floor while my aunt was in the Ladies room. Upon coming out of the restroom, she began to yell at me for what I was doing, telling me to stop. I didn't know that what I was doing was a problem. What I was doing wasn't wrong. However, I guess it was inappropriate, from her point of view, to turn somersaults in the middle of the floor in the bus terminal. How else does a child entertain themselves? They find something to do that is creative. I was merely doing what kids do - attempting to create a way to have fun. Fun is what you make it to be at seven years of age. In the adult world, the behavior was seen as immature. I can say, probably, it was. What do you expect from a seven year old, I ask? I was acting as and doing what a seven year old boy does. Boys at such a young age aren't thinking of right and wrong, whether someone is looking or not, or whether the behavior is immature or not. A child at seven is merely trying to amuse him- or herself and making every effort to have fun.

A child should be permitted to be a child. In today's world adults want their children to grow up too quickly. Parents want their children to be in preschool at two years of age. According to some adults, their child should be learning something or at least be getting a head start regarding their education. When did it become necessary to educate children at two years of age? Why can't they enjoy their childhood, which is having fun with no responsibilities? Of course, as they get older, age appropriate responsibilities should be given to them for the purpose of personal development.

As I pondered that scene in the bus station that day in Cheyenne so many years ago, I reached the conclusion that I was just being a child, enjoying the moment. I was not hurting anyone. In fact, I am sure that there were those who were getting a kick out of me as I was trying to entertain myself with those somersaults in the middle of the floor. It was an activity that may be considered immature for a seven year old by the adult or parent, but not by the child. As an adult, far removed from that scene, I am able to look at it from a different vantage point. It really wasn't an immature act for me. I believe that I was acting my age. As a seven year old, why would I think that doing a somersault in the floor was immature. There would be no reason for me to think or even comprehend, most likely, what immaturity was. What is immaturity? There are many sources one can find to determine the definition of immaturity. Let's look at a few.

Immaturity

- having or showing emotional or intellectual development appropriate to someone younger
- acting in or exhibiting a childish manner
- not behaving in a way that is as calm and wise as people expect from someone your age

Source (https://dictionary.cambridge.org)

Do you notice a common thread that is weaved between these definitions. All three point to behavior that is indicative of someone who is younger, let's say, those individuals who are in the development years. Let's say these would be the ages from two through eighteen years of age, given the fact that in many states, eighteen is when a person is considered an adult. That might be true with the number, but not necessarily with emotions or psychological understanding. Another possible term that may be used especially in our culture today, would be emotional intelligence. Emotional Intelligence is the capacity of individuals to recognize their own and other people's emotions, to discriminate between different feelings and label them appropriately, and to use emotional information to guide thinking and behavior. We are speaking in general, not from the view point of all. You will find some teenagers that are quite mature for their age, most likely as a result of growing up within a very structured family of origin. *(This could also occur out of necessity, having been put into a situation that required the person to "grow up fast" in order to survive or take care of others.)* There are some instances where the person is just mature by nature. So to expect a person 18 years of age and younger to possess a high degree of emotion intelligence is outside the normal realm of expectations.

Considering the age level of a person, we would then need to know what is age appropriate. It is in this level of thinking where common sense should be exercised. For example, are we to expect a five-year-old to understand everything that they are told? Of course not! A five-year-old does not have the brain that is able to comprehend what a twenty-year-old should comprehend, though, there are exceptions to the norm. I was just watching the news recently and there was a story about an 11-year-old boy who was starting college. He is a child prodigy who is the first student his age to receive a full scholarship at Southern University. His major is physics. I then did a little research and found other 11-year-old children who had graduated college at that same age of 11. Can you imagine that? It is true! I am sure that these 11-year-old pre-teens, though geniuses, still have areas of emotional immaturity in their lives because of their chronological age. It still would be expected that a child so young would be acting in ways that would indicate their chronological age range despite their intellectual abilities. Would you expect a seventeen year old to throw a tantrum? The answer would be no. However, many seventeen-year-olds who say they want to be adults, do throw tantrums. We can even say that individuals much older than seventeen throw tantrums. You would expect a thirty year old to be able to make a decision on what they should do in a given situation or at least to be familiar with a process in order to come to a decision regarding the situation, but many cannot.

We all have our ideas of what maturity is supposed to look like and at what age. It appears that immaturity for many is relative. To some extent, the previous statement might be correct. There are some general expectations with various ages, however, there is a degree of relativity or bias that definitely could play into the reasoning of how one views immaturity. Most older individuals who could be identified as being immature, might be blind to their condition.

Let's take a journey into the workplace. As stated earlier, I was a District Manager for almost twenty five years in municipal government. I experienced immaturity in the workplace with regularity. I would even refer to myself at times as the manager of daycare operations. I really want you to envision what I am saying. Some of you might have even experienced what I am now talking about. Imagine a group of toddlers in a room crying about the fact that they didn't get the toys they wanted to play with; some complaining about going outside; others wanting to play cowboys and Indians; still others yelling and throwing a tantrum because they want to eat a snack. Those who are daycare workers probably have experienced the aforementioned scenarios. It is not much different at some work locations. I can easily talk about my work locations and what took place in them.

There were guys always complaining about the job assignment given to them; another would complain about the weather and why they can't go out; others didn't want to leave the shop on time; still others wanted to grab a coffee before they got to the work site. There were guys who were complaining and griping about the fact that I was making them work too much and that other districts weren't working like us. These types of complaints were continuous over my entire managerial career. What was the key to handling such immaturity? My faith!

I must say that some of the individuals who were complaining were even proclaiming to be believers. The questions, in light of what we are talking about, is how do we handle the immaturity of others and how do we avoid becoming immature or exhibiting behavior like theirs?

These questions can be asked from both the managerial side as well as the worker side of the coin. If we apply our definition of immaturity to the individuals who were complaining all the time, we would see that employees in the workplace are acting the same way as the toddlers at the daycare. The ages of the workers, however, ranged between twenty-five and sixty-five years of age. What I had to learn was not to allow myself to get emotionally caught up in their complaining. I had a responsibility to get the assignments completed and they were the individuals who needed to get them done. Even though their complaining felt quite personal in nature, I had to not look at what they were saying as being personal. I believe that is the first principle we need to learn in the workplace when it comes to personal maturity. Don't receive everything that is said as personal even though they are intending it to be, in most instances.

As a manager, I am not trying to be friends with the workers. I am not trying to win their affection. I am not trying to get them to suck up to me and to get them to like me. That is not why I am there in the workplace in the capacity that I was operating out of. I am there to get a job done and to serve, at the time, the people of Philadelphia. I needed to do that to the best of my ability. My focus then had to be on something higher than the employees. The focus had to be on doing whatever task that needed to be completed that day. I also needed to be doing the job to the best of my ability for the glory of God. The faith component was such a major part of my life and was helping me from taking things personally.

How is it that men who are older than me behave like children? And the complaining was only one part of it. There was the hiding out in the afternoons, the irresponsibility of not completing jobs, the intentional forgetfulness of details, the purposeful sabotage of equipment as well as the negligent use of it. There was the habitual lateness by some; the liquid lunches that altered afternoon attitudes at times, and the AWOLS that were a constant problem for some. There was also the not owning up to the accidents involving city vehicles. There were the feeble weak excuses as to why things weren't done and the constant creative ways of trying to get out of doing work. All these descriptions of behaviors evolve out of immaturity as well as irresponsibility. Why? They involve elements of immaturity that are associated with childlike behavior. They also involve the childish attitudes that are behind the behaviors.

Immaturity can be part of a mindset not just a behavior. A mindset that causes people to make decisions that are childlike in nature. Decisions that are made without considering others or the ramifications of those decisions regarding self and others. A childish mind is a mind that doesn't fully think from all the angles. Notice a child and what he/she does: They are extremely selfish.

A child wants his/her way. They only see what they want. They are unable to see why they can't have what they want and how it might not be the best for them. Children aren't looking at the logical reasoning behind what they do, in most cases. The world centers around them; they expect you to move when they tell you and to do what they tell you to do. This is the behavior of a child. What is so amazing about these characteristics is that they are permitted by parents in many of the homes across America. I am quite certain that many of these children who have come out of homes that allowed the behavior that is exhibited in their lives as adults is directly related to what they did as children. Adults who exhibit this behavior are immature. By the way, let's be clear: management is not excluded from such immature behavior. We are able to find immature supervisors and managers at work locations across the country as well. How they stay in their positions, God only knows!

If we are exhibiting immaturity in the workplace or aspects of childish behavior on a personal level, God wants us to change. How does this change happen for us? Here is the interesting thing: it can start when we are confronted by people who point it out to us. We must be willing to receive what they say and sift it through the grid of the Holy Spirit. If we see it in other people, then as a believer and a person who is to be salt and light, God wants us to possibly confront that person or persons in love.

The second quality that God wants to work in us is love. This word love is loosely used and is mostly used in a romantic sense. This love, especially the love that God desires to develop in us, is what is called agape, unconditional love. This love is continuously looking out for the best interest of the other. When this love is implemented toward a co-worker, what is it supposed to look like? How does one show this love to employees when they are being treated wrongly? That is a great question. Here is a tough truth. It doesn't matter how they treat us at the time or our feelings toward them. Our responsibility is to reflect God's love. This love that God has is radical and different. How can those at our place of employment experience this love that is so life changing, if we never allow God to show it through us? How can this be accomplished if we are constantly bitter, angry, hateful and distant because of the action of others? How can they experience this radical life-giving love if our deportment is like theirs or if we are being duplicitous? Jesus always moved toward sinners. He even loved and offered salvation to the church leadership who opposed Him continuously. Jesus loved when people were hard to love, in the midst of physical, psychological and emotional abuse. We see Jesus in Matt. 9:9-12 inviting Matthew, who is a tax collector, to be a disciple. We then see Jesus having dinner with tax collectors and sinners at Matthew's house. This was a no-no for a Jew to be having a meal with such individuals who were considered to be sinners and virtually nobodies. Jesus loved, no matter who the person was. He was loving the most hated people in the land at that time, the tax collectors. Why? Because His purpose was to bring salvation to the Jews as well as to the Gentiles. We even are able to see that the sinners wanted to be around Jesus because He was receptive to them as individuals despite the condition of their lives. His acceptance of them and the display of love is what ultimately changed their hearts. Despite the difficulties with the individuals whom with we interact with in the workplace, we still need to respond from a position of love.

Immaturity can be seen at every level of the work environment. As long as there are people, there will be immaturity. Some people might only have immaturity in a specific area of their being while others exhibit immaturity in their entire person. We must be able to tell the difference and respond accordingly. We are not able to know why the immaturity is present in people, we just know that it appears on a regular basis. If we can identify it in people and be willing to help them to grow, then we have done them a favor and enhanced their lives. We have helped them to be a better person which will ultimately help them to influence others in a different way. If we are open to receiving from others with regard to areas of immaturity in our own lives, we have the opportunity to grow if we allow what they give us to change us. Both directions are vital for us to develop Christlikeness.

Day care is where you find a lot of immaturity. It is expected to be found there and is expected to be present for quite some time there. The reason being is that daycare is for children who are in a certain age range. Immaturity is part of the child's world at that stage. They don't know the world yet from a deeper developed thought process. Their brains, in general, are not able to function at such a high level. This type of childish behavior is not to be, nor should it be expected to be, found in the workplace; but yet it exists. For some who are immature, they cannot help it due to a mental disorder or some type of psychological issue. For others, emotionally, they never grew up or developed, possibly due to factors out of their control. Still others, they are just childish in nature and chose to remain in that condition. There are just some adults who continue to have the mindset of a child. Many of these individuals have been given a pass in life. People have let behaviors continue without any kind of repercussions. This allowance or permission for such a person to continue in their behavior without confrontation is a dis-service to the person and those around them. As a believer in a work situation or environment where we are experiencing such behavior, we need to be willing to be used to speak truth and to be a catalyst for change. We have to be willing to take a risk. God places us at different work locations so that people can experience Jesus. So the real question becomes, "Will I allow Him to show up in me?"

In I Corinthians 13, which is the "love chapter" that many couples will have read at their weddings. if they knew the real truth and context behind what Paul is writing, this passage probably wouldn't be used anymore. Paul is actually rebuking the Corinthians about their lack of love. He is ripping into them about the things that they were allowing and doing that was not showing the love that God wanted to be displayed. He confronts them with this "love chapter" by telling them what real love looks like. He says in 13:11, "When I was a child I talked as a child, I thought like a child, I reasoned like a child, But when I became a man, I put away childish things."

If I am developing in love, that means I am becoming a mature man or a mature woman. Love, when it is increased, increases maturity. Can you now see how all the things that people do in the workplace can help us develop in love?. When we grow in love, we are growing in maturity. Childish ways of talking, thinking, and reasoning are being replaced with mature (adult) ways of handling situations. Someone must be the grown up in the room! Why not have it be me or you? As believers, we should always be seeking to be the grown up in the room. When Jesus shows up, the grown-up has arrived.

Chapter 5

ENCOUNTERING DIFFICULT PEOPLE

1982 WAS A GREAT YEAR. WHY? IT WAS THE YEAR THAT I GRADUATED from Pennsylvania State University. I was fresh out of college with no job and no leads for any jobs. It was time for a summer vacation this particular year, and much deserved, especially since being in school the previous 3 summers as well as the past 3 years without any break. It would be nice to be able not to do anything and to have my brain relax. So my summer was off to a wonderful, slow start. Finally, in early August, my dad told me to go see the council person in our area. The council person gave me a lead that led me to a job with Awbury Arboretum which is located in the Germantown section of Philadelphia. When I got hired, there would only be two of us who were working there, myself as a grounds worker along with an Arborist who was my supervisor. It was at my very first job out of college where I learned how to drive a stick shift truck. This new skill would lead to me personally getting a stick shift car - a Cougar - that I ended up having for several years. My stint at the Arboretum didn't last long, five weeks to be exact. Another job opportunity presented itself, and I gladly accepted it. It was a groundskeeper position with a private contractor, but located on the property of a Federal Government installation. It was a research center located in Mount Airy, which is located in the northwest section of Philadelphia. There I was involved in all kinds of maintenance, including doing things indoors, such as moving furniture as well as mopping and waxing floors. It was at this job where I cut my teeth in the working world and where I would encounter my first difficult person.

As a 21-year-old employee, fresh out of college for only 6 months, you are not expecting to run into a person who is blatant with their racism; let's call him Tim. Tim was older than me, somewhat quiet, but seem to have a chip on his shoulder most of the time. Tim always appeared to have an attitude. I would work with this person for 3 ½ years. Now that I look back, I realize that there were many difficult days, especially when we had an assignment together without the foreman. How did I keep my head on straight? How did I survive this person who clearly practiced his racism, as well as verbalized it in the workplace on several occasions?

As I look back on this time in my life over 35 years ago, I can see that it was the presence of God actively working in my life at the time, keeping me patient and keeping me in self-control mode. Learning what being a disciple of Christ was while in Campus Crusade for Christ on the college campus of Penn State had prepared me to deal with this person in the workplace at 21 years of age. What were some of the things he would do, you might ask? That is a good question! Notice I used the term blatant earlier in a description of him. That term means something done openly and unashamedly. Tim would have an air of "being better than everyone else." The attitude of "you are nobody to me" was just evident when in his presence. There were times that he just would not answer you when talking to him or would be sarcastic. There were times he would try to be the superior one in front of the scientists when we were doing a job. There were times he stated that he didn't like black people. He would always want to do the good jobs and have me do the undesirable ones. The other factor that most likely came into play was that I was a college graduate and he just made it through high school. There would be a point in time in my job experience where I would encounter being called a "Nigger" by Tim. There was no discipline given nor anything done about it. Welcome to the real world!

This was my new experience in life. Yet, God was faithful to keep me there until He saw fit to move me. I am sure that some of you know what it is like to have someone you work with every day, who doesn't particularly care for you because of skin tone, ethnicity, sex, weight, etc., or who just disliked you for no apparent reason at all. No matter what type of prejudice that is encountered by a person, the one factor that can't be forgotten is that the root of it is with the heart. It is what comes out of the inside of the person that has an effect on us. What I was encountering with Tim was hatred, prejudice and meanness. These traits were part of who he was as a person and had been instilled in him for several years. Little did I know, there would be a power in me that I didn't know was being exhibited at the time. As a new full-time employee in the work world, I thought that this was behavior that I needed to learn how to deal with on the job.

Tim could be described as a difficult person; his character was one that was least to be desired. For a man who was in his thirties to display an ignorance that is still displayed today by individuals who have never learned that some of the things they say or do to others can be offensive and racist, was not mature nor acceptable. Please understand that racism is expressed by people of all ethnic groups. My experience with Tim helped me to understand how to dwell in a situation with him without losing my mind or going crazy. I was directly rubbing up against a person who did not like me or anybody who looked like me. The thing in my favor was that I had a God who loved me, was there with me and was teaching me something about me, about Him and about Tim. There were times in my heart, I wanted to hit Tim. There were times I wish somebody would do something with this guy. What I was learning, but didn't know it at the time, was that the workplace can't control people's attitudes. The supervisor or leadership can discipline for violations of policy, but cannot regulate attitude. I was either going to learn how to live every day with this person or I would have to try to find another job, but it never entered my mind to change jobs.

In Chapter 2 we talked about self-awareness. Self-awareness is crucial in navigating difficult people. A person should know their "buttons", especially those that set them off. There are buzz words or actions that can be displayed by people that will immediately cause you to react. If you know that, what do you do about it in order to change it? Do you still continue to just allow the same buttons to be pushed? There are those people in the workplace who will never change and will remain difficult. Who then is the one to break the cycle? If you are the one being affected by the behavior, you are the one responsible for allowing the behavior to affect you. As a believer who is encountering a difficult person, it is essential that one examine his/her own heart first. What do we make the first priority in the workplace when we have a problem with a person?

Fast forward to when I started working with the City of Philadelphia. My first few years was as a Grounds Worker 1. I did everything grounds-related, which included cutting grass, cutting and trimming shrubs and small trees, working on ball fields, picking up paper, emptying trashcans, planting flowers, etc. As a 26-year-old entering the city workforce, I now had a job that would be pretty stable as well as pave a way for advancement since I had a college degree. However, I would now encounter some interesting employees. Some of these guys I would describe as being really "out there in left field." Some were alcoholics, some drug addicts; some were high school dropouts; some were professional street philosophers; some were jailhouse lawyers, and some were escape artists who were allergic to work. There were very few who worked hard. All these guys were older than me. They were set in their ways and knew the system they were a part of and had been for many years. I quickly found out that a couple of these guys were very difficult. It wasn't racism this time. It was the lack of productivity during the work day. In other words, I was being told I worked too hard and I was messing up their groove. Fortunately I didn't work with these guys every day. It was myself and a classmate of mine from high school who were assigned to a specific area known as Logan Circle. This would be my location until my brief stint at the Greenhouse as a gardener. I found it quite amazing that guys would make it their job to get out of work and had become quite good at it.

I found a new challenge with the interactions with this particular group of individuals. Was I going to become like them - gravitating to the status quo of trying to get out of work in order to be accepted - or would I stand alone with my own work ethic risking the flack I would have to take for not acclimating to their position on work? The failure to become like them would undoubtedly lead to their resentment and hatred toward me, and that is exactly what happened. The common denominator among them was attitude. Standing alone in the workplace is an essential quality that is needed as a believer. Learning to not give in and go against your convictions is a major part of ultimately being able to establish credibility with your character. Isn't it the character of the person that is important? This is how credibility is earned in the workplace. It has to be displayed through the character that is shown when the heat is turned up because of the difficult person's attitudes. Standing alone, like I had to do in the aforementioned situation, will bring criticism along with the attitudes. The criticism will be negative. There will also be false accusations with it as well. But how do you handle it – that is, people, saying all kinds of things, making up things, declaring things as if they are true about you.? There really is nothing that you can do about it. There is nothing you can do to control it. You cannot keep people from saying things, thinking things or spreading falsehoods about you. You must put in place the following principle "No Defense, No Attack."

Trying to defend yourself is going to get you frustrated, angry and have you doing and saying things you shouldn't. This is a situation where we need to be like Jesus. He didn't try to defend Himself. Jesus, who could have called down angels from heaven to zap all of His difficult people, didn't do that. He focused on what He was called to do with his sight being the Cross. What is our focus on when it comes to those difficult people who are lying on us, criticizing us harshly, making up accusations about us and constantly having our energy being drawn toward their negative dispositions? They would be considered enemies from a biblical perspective, and what are we to do with them? Love them! Yes, once again, our faith enters into the equation. Recognizing who we are in Christ and Who we work for on a higher scale enables us to keep on our center, that being more like Christ.

I am reminded of a Scripture in Matthew 5.43-45 where Jesus is speaking on various issues while in the midst of an audience including His disciples. He says "You have heard that it was said "Love your neighbor and hate your enemy; But I tell you: Love your enemies and pray for those who persecute you, that you may be sons of your Father in heaven. He causes the sun to rise on the evil and the good, and sends rain on the righteous and unrighteous." In our identification with Christ, the treatment by evil people will be present in our lives and there will be different forms of it. Notice what Jesus said: There will be persecution in our lives and the main ingredient in handling it is through prayer. Pray for the person and the situation. Why? Maybe, at least for the believer, God will give us wisdom on how to approach the person who is our enemy. Let's be honest: prayer isn't usually the first thing we do when it comes to an enemy. Praying for an enemy requires a discipline that is outside of us and is directly tied into love, specifically the agape-type of love that we are called to display. It is from a place of love that God wants to operate and He is continually instilling in us, through His Spirit, the ability to do the same, as well as the long-suffering attributes that are needed for us to be strengthened.

As you might expect, many of the difficult people whom I would encounter in my career would be when I became a District Manager. As I recall, my first assignment was in the West Philadelphia and Southwest Philadelphia areas. The primary park in West Philadelphia was Cobbs Creek Parkway. My development as a manager who had to deal with difficult people on a daily basis would begin there. Difficult people in the workplace come in all shapes, sizes, and colors. Although the term I just used in the previous sentence can be literal, it is also figurative. Difficulties know no boundaries. There are people who will have multiple issues and those who might have just one issue. I will attempt to show different characteristics associated with each person with whom I interacted.

There was Denny, who was the supervisor at the time when I became a District Manager. He was much older than me and had been working for many years with Fairmount Park. I was in my early thirties and fresh in my new role. You would think that Denny would extend his hand to help me, wouldn't you? Well, not so! Denny was old school, stuck in his way of doing things and how he wanted things to be. Denny was not one to reveal information concerning the job. He reminded me of the cartoon character, Secret Squirrel. Simply speaking, with all of the experience that Denny had, he did not have a desire to really coach me or aid me in understanding the ropes in the district. I was left to figure things out, for the most part. I believed that in his mind, he thought to himself, "He is the college boy, let him figure it out." If I had come into the situation acting like I knew everything, then I could understand his attitude. However, I came in the situation humble, willing to allow the supervisors to have input into things. I was the one that was in the middle of a learning curve. It wasn't Denny that I came to depend on; it was a tree foreman who helped me to navigate this new territory I was now immersed in called park management. The experience and assistance from a tree foreman would help me to understand how to navigate the new waters that I was now swimming. This early gift of God in the field would be needed as I began this journey in management. Denny was aloof and resentful because I was this new young kid on the block who would change things. Was he correct? Of course! Anytime you have someone new in a leadership role in the workplace, there will be change that will come with it at some point in time. Denny was selfish, guarded, and very closed-minded to new things. Our interaction at times was tense, unpredictable, and frustrating. In the midst of his behavior, I had to be the one to adjust to the situation with him. Learning how to be flexible with the person's attitude and still be able to get the production of work out of them was one of the challenging aspects of the job.

Then there was my secretary, who I will call Angela. Angela was new to Fairmount Park, but not new to working in the city. She had come from the Managing Director's office, having transferred from that department to ours. Our interaction was more frequent than with the supervisor because of the necessity of having to talk with her several times a day about many issues that would come up. The nature of her job required my attention. There were the phone calls, messages, correspondence, reports, and any other work assignments that were office-related or that fell under her job description.

The problem with Angela was that she knew everything about everything. Up until this point, I had never encountered such a person. It didn't matter what subject, she was an expert. When giving her work assignments that needed to be done in a specific way, she would do it her way. I would tell her that what she had done wasn't acceptable and needed to be done over. There would be a disagreement on her part as to why it needed to be changed. There was a continual presence of an attitude that she was one that knew best how things should be done; her way was always the best way. She was stubborn, unyielding, rigid and blind to her weaknesses. Despite the battles that we had pertaining to work assignments, I had to learn patience in the midst of still having to discipline her when necessary.

How about our next difficult person, whom I will call Kareem. Kareem was a ground maintenance worker who was transferred from another district to mine. As I think about it, my district was known for having all the trouble makers; all the problem children were sent west. Kareem had some issues in the other district, so I knew he was going to be a problem. He wasn't there that long before he showed his real self - I actually used part of what he did in an earlier chapter. I will say this: Through his continued negative behavior of lateness and being A.W.O.L, I was put in the position of keeping track of what he was doing daily. I would go in the back room where the guys would come in and wait or mark the attendance sheet. Starting time was at 7 AM. My office was in the front of the building while their entrance was in the back of the building. Even though I was focusing on Kareem, I had to deal with the other guys who were also coming in late. I was placed in the position of disciplining the employees who were continuously late, but Kareem was the worst offender. One day Kareem was extremely late. In fact, he was no longer late at the point he had come to work. If an employee doesn't call in by 8 AM, he or she is now considered Absent Without Leave. I confronted Kareem out in the yard as he was walking down the driveway. He walked up to my face and said " You ain't nothing but an Uncle Tom

Nigger!" How about that one! I had been called the N-word before as I shared with you in a previous chapter, but I never been called the N-word by an African-American. Welcome to the wonderful world of management! Being one of the managers at the time, the only one who was African-American, I was quick to find out that I would encounter difficult people from all sides. This would include the public as well. It didn't matter what color or nationality or gender; difficult people are difficult people. Kareem eventually was fired, not because of that incident - which was insubordination - but because I had accumulated so much paperwork on him for the lateness and the A.W.O.L.'s through progressive discipline that his actions finally caught up with him. He had fired himself; I just kept the paperwork. Kareem was rude, disrespectful, ignorant, unwilling to listen to reason, unwilling to change behavior and extremely arrogant. Believe it or not, I gave him more than enough time to change, but he didn't value the grace that was being extended to him.

I will share one more person that I encountered my first few years in management. We had a new employee, let's call her Katie. Katie was just starting off as a grounds worker with the City of Philadelphia. There is a 6-month probationary period before you become permanent. Katie started off like gangbusters, doing everything she was asked. I had started to hear some negative things about her work, but because I am not out with the crew on a daily basis, I didn't know on a personal level what she was doing or not doing. One day during her probationary period, I caught her sleeping in the truck during work hours. I woke her up and asked what was up. Of course, I got the typical answer, "I was on break." Anyway, I let it go. She could have been fired at that point without

a process since she was on probation. Well, Katie became permanent after the 6 months were over, and then we saw and experienced a dramatic change in her. Katie became my new problem
child. Her attitude was absolutely horrible and now she didn't want
to do her assignments. There was always some kind of problem;
and by the way, there was some more sleeping. I then began to ask
myself "What did you do?" I should have been able to anticipate
what I now was experiencing from what I saw that day in the truck
with her sleeping. I should have let her go that day. Just to let you
know, her actions eventually caught up with her several years later
in another district and she was fired because of her behavior. I truly
must say, for someone to lose a government job, you really have to
be someone who doesn't care about anything. It truly is difficult to
get rid of a difficult person in a government job.

As I think about my interaction with Katie, she had two sides
to her. There was a nice, charming side and a mean, cutting side.
There was a term that I would hear people use growing up: "nice-
nasty." That would be a good description of Katie. She could really
turn the charm on when she got in trouble and would have you
feeling sorry for her. I had allowed that nice, charming side to blind
me of the other side. My weakness then, and still is today in many
instances, is to give people the benefit of the doubt. I do my best
to believe the best about a person in spite of witnessing the worst.
Katie was manipulative, calculating, smooth-talking and always
looking out for herself. I am still able to remember the times that
I brought her into my office, closed the door, and tried to help her
with some personal issues. Yes, I even shared Jesus with her at a
time that she was going through some heavy things. Apparently,
she didn't allow Jesus to help her with her struggles.

The difficult people mentioned above were part of the beginning of my journey. I encountered these four individuals, as well as some others during those 3 1/2 years at Cobbs Creek. I then found myself at a new location, that being the Horticulture Center and Arboretum in the Belmont section of Philadelphia. There I would encounter another set of employees who would also help me to change and to grow in my walk with Christ through their challenging ways and behaviors. Since there were not a lot of employees on site at the Horticulture Center, I will not use any names, but will share some experiences that will still bring out the behaviors of people.

It was while in school studying counseling that I was able to gain valuable insight on some of my employees. I needed to do several analysis profiles as part of my counseling work for school. I was able to use most of the employees at the Horticulture Center for this purpose. I needed to have them take a questionnaire that would then give me a clinical report. I would then meet with them to give them the results of the report. The analysis is Christian-based and measured the traits in their temperaments. We were then able to see the behaviors that were present with the person because of their trying to meet the needs of their particular temperament traits. I was able to see how each of the employees was wired. Having this information helped me to understand their behavior. I was able to then make adjustments to how they were acting and not allow their behavior to impact me in a negative way.

There was one person who had indirect behavior; this means that the person asks for something and then when it is given, refuses it. I'll give you an example: If Person A comes into the room and sees a group talking, Person A would not join the group unless they are asked. If asked, they would join in and be fine. If they weren't asked, they would stand there and wait. If never asked, they would become upset because they weren't asked. But they would not join the group on their own. This is an example of indirect behavior. I dealt with a person like this but, at the time, didn't understand why they were exhibiting this behavior; but it was "in" them to behave that way. They are *"wafflers"* and tend to go back and forth naturally as part of who they are.

There were a few people who were extremely opinionated. They had something to say about everything and everybody. They would say things like: "This person didn't do this right" or "This person should have done this" or "This person had no business doing this." It didn't matter how or who did what, there was always a problem. I came to understand that people who tend to complain about how everybody else didn't do things right are controllers and want to be in charge of everything; they know better than everybody else. Their ideas and their way of doing things is always better, These individuals have aspects of narcissism in them. Interacting with them is quite challenging, but can be done effectively. Standing your ground with a narcissist that is in a position under you can be dealt with by recognizing them for their ideas while helping them to value others' opinions as much as their own.

Have you ever run into a person who is always angry? They just walk and talk in ways that indicate displeasure with people and life on a regular basis. The glass is always half empty; their lens is one of negativity all the time. The world is against them and someone is always out to get them. Individuals that are like this, believe it or not, tend to be like that all their lives; it is just in them to be negative. This is indicative of a person whose temperament is predominantly melancholy. They interact with the world through the grid of negativity and they see people the same way.

Then you have those people that are just jerks. They are just individuals that don't care about what they say or do. They do not think before they talk. They just come out with stuff at the wrong time and they don't care who hears what is said. If they want to say something, they will say it and no one can stop them. Unfortunately, there are usually jerks in the workplace. The definition of a jerk is, "a contemptibly obnoxious person." These are individuals that are very immature and act, in many cases, worse than a child. Interaction with them requires direct involvement on occasions, but truth and confrontation when appropriate. The typical behavior by a jerk should not be tolerated and, if in the workplace, the behavior should be dealt with directly.

As time went on, I encountered more difficult people, but many of the experiences were similar in nature to the ones already mentioned. It doesn't matter where you are, the difficulties will be the same because people are the same no matter where you are. Yes, we are all unique and different, but all people fall into combinations of five different temperaments which are melancholy, sanguine, choleric, phlegmatic, and supine. All people in the world, over 7 Billion, will fall somewhere in straight or in some combination of these five temperaments. Difficulties will come about due to the behaviors that are being used to fulfill the traits that exist in each of the temperaments. As one is familiarized with the temperaments, the associated behaviors can be identified, which will then bring clearer understanding about the person who is difficult.

In the previous chapter I talked about the importance of understanding people. A major part to getting along with difficult people is to understand how each person ticks. It sounds like work, doesn't it? Well, it is work! But think of the heartaches and the stress it will save over the years in the workplace if we are aware of the dynamics involved in understanding people. From a biblical perspective, it will open our eyes to see God move in powerful ways both in our lives and the lives of whose with whom we interact.

Chapter 6

HANDLING CONFLICT

IS IT POSSIBLE FOR EVERYTHING TO GO WELL IN OUR LIVES, ESPECIALLY in the workplace? If things aren't expected to go well in our homes where we reside, then why would we expect our places of employment to be any different? When you consider the animal kingdom, there are always times of conflict. In many situations, especially with some of the larger animals like bucks or lions, they actually fight to determine the outcome of the conflict. With animals, the conflict usually is centered around territorial issues such as a certain area of land or a female of their species. If there is conflict among the animal kingdom where animals are not able to evaluate a situation with the complexity of human minds, you would think that humans, with the capacity to dissect information in a complex way, would be able to have less conflict with each other. This is not the case. Conflict is inevitable when you have more than one person present in relationship, whether just as friends or as co-workers. Though conflict is something that occurs normally, the question that remain is, "Why is there conflict? We all need to understand that conflict evolves out of relationship; in fact, conflict is part of life and has been part of humankind since the fall in the garden by Adam and Eve. At the point when sin entered into the lives of humankind, the capacity of experiencing conflict came with it. How conflict is managed, however, is another story. When you consider how two people differ in their thinking, their approach to life, their handling of impromptu situations, as well as their perspective on various aspects of life, there will be differing viewpoints. The process of bumping against each others differing opinions, positions, goals, perspectives, dreams, values and ambitions is what challenges us to communicate why we feel those differences. The animal kingdom does not have the ability to cognitively assess and communicate the differences the way humans are designed to do.

Let's consider how human beings are made in God's image. He gave every person a mind and it is to be used to think. Isn't it interesting how we all think differently? Though many of us think and do agree on several issues, the point that I am making is that we have free will when it comes to thinking. Our minds have the capacity to go anywhere. We already talked about how our minds are able to exhibit creativity. The mind has the capacity to establish positions on various subjects, issues and viewpoints; it is the computer that God has given to every person. These human computers have different capacities when it comes to processing information, more specifically, how that information is processed. The way that men and women process information is totally different. Such differences need to be considered when having a conversation, especially because of the potential for conflict to arise. The minds of many are constantly in motion, hardly ever stopping to rest. The mind is able to remember things that have happened, in the short term as well as the long term. When considering all the information that is in a person's mind, it is truly amazing. But when you add relationships as well as the degree of interaction in those relationships, there will undoubtedly be conflict. There is a collision of viewpoints and perspectives. The question to ask is whether there is a problem with the individuals having different opinions or, rather, approaches to the issue at hand. The answer to that question is no. Where there are people, there *will* be different perspectives and opinions. Developing a skill set to approach people with similar, as well as totally different, perspectives than ours is essential to successfully navigating the waters of life, no matter where we are: home, work, church, civic groups, game activities, etc.

It has been my experience in the workplace, that many employees bring their problems to work with them. Many don't know how to separate what has taken place in their personal lives from their work environment. Their emotions from the event that transpired prior to work, or even on the way to work, have carried over into the relationships in the workplace. There now will be a flare up or infliction of their frustration onto the individuals with whom they work, and if a person is addicted to drugs or alcohol, the drama from that person is exacerbated. The behavior will present itself in the workplace in various ways through their behavior, which can even include insubordination with the supervisor. There were numerous times over the years as a manager, as well as a regular employee, in which the behaviors of an employee appeared to be intensified due to substance abuse but, of course, couldn't be proven. Many times, the behavior was on the borderline; the behavior displayed was quite inappropriate, but did not seem to hinder their job performance. There were many times that individuals were close, but I couldn't really justify sending them to 19th Street, our facility where drug testing would take place. The problem that also hindered the ability of sending someone to 19th street was having a second person to verify the behavior of the employee. If a second person, usually another manger or supervisor, wasn't available, it became almost impossible to send the person for testing. I remember a situation where an employee came in the office early in the morning and appeared to be acting strangely. There was alcohol on his breath. I was going to have him taken down to 19th St., but when I called to see if I could do this, I was asked if I saw him drinking? The answer, of course, was no. I was then asked if he was functional; for the most part, the answer was yes. To make a long story short, he didn't have to go to 19th St. I was angry because I was trying to do my job and wasn't allowed to do it.; I was having a conflict. Unfortunately, I did not agree with the rules, but had to follow them. Even though I was in conflict with Human Resources, there was nothing I could do. There were several situations over the years where I had to let things go, despite knowing that I now had grounds to have an employee disciplined. My attitude could have been to let everything from that point go, but I still had a job to do and things for which I had to be responsible.

There were many conflicts that took place over the years, There were conflicts between the employees, employees and management, and employees with the public. If I can be totally honest, conflict was a weekly occurrence. What I mean by that is, there was at least one major conflict every week. There was drama all the time, it was part of the job. From a management perspective drama, unfortunately, this was most definitely true. I wish that I could say that it wasn't but, as I've stated previously, it is the nature of people. There will always be at least one employee, if not more, that will cause conflict regularly. When there are individuals that are immature and do not know how to handle themselves well emotionally, there will be conflict. As stated already, we have conflict as a result of different ways of thinking, which is how God made us. The problem is how the conflict is managed and how one sees the other person in light of the conflict. If conflict is going to occur, is it possible for it to be minimized? I believe that is the key, not only in the workplace, but in general. Understanding where the person is on the issue, why they feel a certain way, and how they arrived at the position that they have, are all key factors to understanding the person. Agreement may not be necessary at the point where you are with them. Understanding might well be what is needed until there has been some discussion on the matter.

Conflict in the workplace can be toxic, especially if it occurs regularly. It can be like a cancer, eating away at the productivity of good employees. Only one person is needed to turn over the apple cart and bring about havoc in the workplace. A person, whether willfully causing problems or conflict among other employees or unintentionally, must be dealt with in order to keep order in the workplace. It is necessary that a manager enters into the situations of employees in order to keep order. That means there must be a proactive approach with the employees who are in conflict in order to attempt to keep the peace. I believe that it doesn't matter whether the conflict is something that has occurred at work or not. If the workplace atmosphere is impacted in a negative way or if employees are affected, the situation must be handled before the environment becomes toxic. When conflict is allowed to fester and grow, there can be a lot of toxicity that will come along with the neglect of handling the situation promptly. There have been several employees whom I have seen over the years who were not disciplined appropriately and went on to cause havoc no matter where they were placed. To be honest, especially when the merger came about in 2011 between Fairmount Park and The Department of Recreation, what became apparent after a short period of time was that Recreation didn't really handle the employees who were problems; they were merely transferred to another location. Moving a person from one location to another doesn't change a person's behavior. They will continue to do the same things that they were doing in the prior location. The only difference is that they are in another location under the supervision of another person. How has the behavior been changed? How has the conflict that the employee has been producing in the workplace been altered? Moving a person is not the answer; it avoids the handling of the real problem and pushes it off to someone else. It actually sets free the supervisor who allowed the person to continue with the behavior. How does that supervisor grow and how does the employee change? Managers who cope this way are not very good managers.

The employee might not have a desire to share personal information if the conflict is outside of the workplace. However, the manager should inform the employee that they must get some help with their problem, should the work environment continue to be toxic. However, when the conflict involves a work-related issue regarding another employee or circumstance, the employee must be immediately confronted without question.

It is imperative that the workplace be an environment that is as safe as possible. What do I mean by the word safe? The work environment, like the home environment, should provide an atmosphere where a person doesn't feel restricted to speak or to express themselves freely. There is a sense of respect as well as acceptance among everyone, an appreciation of what each person brings to the table despite imperfections. When it comes to the cohesiveness, emotional stability, mutual respect and general consideration among the staff, it appears that such a climate in the work environment doesn't often exist in many locations. It appears that employers do not provide a great deal of training when it comes to how to nurture a family atmosphere in which all the members (employees) feel that they are important. Just think if the type of environment it fosters, the potential of the employees' productivity, and the support that could possibly be established among them. In my estimation, one element that I have witnessed quite often, even among supervisors, is favoritism. Favoritism will actually produce the opposite effect, that being a negative environment where employees feel unfairly treated. There were several situations that I witnessed which were precipitated by the supervisor or manager continuously exhibiting favoritism that created conflict among their subordinates. There are many work situations where there are unfair practices that are being implemented by middle management, as well as upper management refusing to handle the subsequent complaints or sweeping them under the rug.

There is one practice that I experienced/witnessed in most of the years of my career, that being blatant nepotism. Despite memos that were given out to all employees, the practice still existed. The interesting thing about it was that the ones who were issuing the regulation were the very ones not abiding by them. There seemed to be a double standard when it came to those who were in upper management. Just think what that does to the moral of most of the employees in the operation. I remember how most of the Fairmount Park employees felt when it came to how management stood their ground and spoke up heavily for the so-called "trust fund" employees as opposed to the regular permanent employees. There was a huge divide with how management, at the time, was fighting for the permanent status of these so-called "trust fund" employees. In other instances, management would hire friends and family to work in positions that they might not have been well-qualified to attain. These types of situations created a great deal of conflict, but it is the type in which employees feel they can have no say-so or feel that it is impossible to win. It is amazing, how much of this practice occurs in city, state, and federal government.

On a personal level, an employee should be given the opportunity to receive training in the area of conflict resolution. Much of conflict is manifested out of anger that is present alongside of a perceived injustice or offense. When that emotion of anger isn't checked, it can then fuel more conflict, especially if the original issue was never resolved. We are able to see that, if a small conflict has never been resolved with a person, other conflicts can be piled on top of the original one. That is why marriages are so messed up by the time couples go to a counselor. The individuals have stock-piled tons of unresolved issues in their relationships and the person now walks around like a ticking time bomb ready to blow up or experience "regurgitation of the mouth" from all the pain brought about by the unresolved issues. When there are multiple piles of unresolved differences among people, and with the numerous people throughout various communities in which anyone participates, no wonder there is so much misery among employees in the workplace! Just add the continuously negative, miserable, obnoxious, immature and angry people (who are just naturally like that,) and you can now see how a highly toxic and stressful workplace develops, not necessarily because of the work but rather because of the people. Most people quit jobs because they no longer want to be around the environment that was created by people, especially a new group of people.

Paul, in Acts, Chapters 12-15 is on his first missionary journey with Barnabas. During that journey, men from various locations would come to where Paul was preaching the gospel and purposely bring about conflict and disruption among the people. These men, who were of the circumcision party (Jews), felt that the Gentiles needed to be circumcised along with their profession of faith and belief in Jesus. This was in contrast to what Paul was preaching, which was that Jesus' finished work at the cross was enough and there was no need for the Gentiles to be circumcised; they were under grace. There were some sharp conflicts, even to the point where Paul was stoned in one of the cities where he was preaching, and left for dead. Paul was working in ministry as an evangelist and a theologian. While at work, he was falsely accused and challenged by those who disliked him and even physically harmed, yet he continued to do the job to which he had been called.

Conflict and pain would always be a part of his life, yet he faced it courageously and honorably. What an example for us to follow! God uses conflict to bring intimacy into the lives of couples who have a close relationship and are expressing love toward each other. In the work environment, God uses conflict to reveal areas in our lives that are in need of healing as well as areas that are in need of a re-calibration. As believers, our attitudes as well as some of our ways and actions can be a hindrance to our witness. God can use conflict to reflect those areas so that they are now on the surface. Once on the surface, the exposed areas of our character that need to be corrected can now be given attention. Do we let conflicts be something that just happens or do we pay attention to why they happen and then allow them to transform our lives? Let's look at Scripture to see the possibilities:

Acts 15:36-41

36 Some time later Paul said to Barnabas, "Let us go back and visit the believers in all the towns where we preached the word of the LORD and see how they are doing." 37 Barnabas wanted to take John, also called Mark, with them, 38 but Paul did not think it wise to take him, because he had deserted them in Pamphylia and had not continued with them in the work. 39 They had such a sharp disagreement that they parted company. Barnabas took Mark and sailed for Cyprus, 40 but Paul chose Silas and left, commended by the believers to the grace of the LORD. 41 He went through Syria and Cilicia, strengthening the churches.

Here in Acts Chapter 15, there is a very serious conflict that occurs between Paul and Barnabas. Barnabas, who had partnered with Paul during his first missionary journey, is about to go on a second with Paul. However, Barnabas, wants to take John Mark who had abandoned them on the first journey. I believe that it is necessary to bring out some points that are present in this conflict that can help us in our lives in general, not just in the workplace.

First, please consider the context: Paul and Barnabas are working together in ministry and their job is preaching and teaching the gospel of Jesus Christ throughout the world. We could say that they are Evangelists. As they are about to embark on another journey, Barnabas wants to take his cousin Mark. Paul is against it, but let's break down the text to get the full application that lies within its meaning:

Principle 1 – Different Opinions – Paul doesn't want to take John Mark because of his abandonment on the first missionary journey. He doesn't trust Mark; he believes that what had happened on the first trip (Acts 13:13) was out of not having a genuine commitment and Paul didn't want to have the same thing happen again. Barnabas, however, sees the situation differently. He believes that Mark is ready this second time around and is willing to give him another opportunity. People today still exhibit these same type of perspectives in various situations.

Principle 2 – Nobody is Wrong – What we see in this conflict - a major conflict - is that both Paul and Barnabas are right. They are seeing the incident that had occurred earlier with John Mark through their individual temperaments. Paul, who appears to exhibit a Type A personality is about getting the job done; he is about results and desires commitment. Barnabas is more relational and people-oriented, a person who is more concerned about a person, in this case specifically, Mark having an opportunity to prove himself again. Barnabas is more forgiving. Remember, Barnabas is the person who went and got Paul in Tarsus and stood up for him in Jerusalem before the Apostles. The issue then is one of preference, not an issue of right or wrong.

Principle 3 – Paul and Barnabas didn't take the position that was being held by the other personally. The opinions expressed by both concerning John Mark going on the trip with them caused sharp disagreement with each other. I must place emphasis here that both of their opinions were based on the truth of the incident. There were two different perspectives, and both were correct. There were no personal attacks toward each other. Being able to focus on the issue without having a lot of emotion and not getting caught up in attempting to speculate motive is of the utmost importance in cases like this.

Principle 4 – A conclusion was determined – It was decided that Barnabas and Paul would part ways. Paul took Silas who had come down to Antioch with them from the mother church in Jerusalem. Barnabas took John Mark who, we know later on in the book of II Corinthians, to be commended by Paul. We actually see the formation of two teams instead of just one team. The decision to part ways benefited the church greatly. Without the different perspectives concerning John Mark, the decision to have two teams might never have happened.

This particular conflict was between two individuals who were partners in their work as well as being friends. Though their sharp disagreement caused the parting of ways between them, it benefited the kingdom overall. Conflict can lead to some amazing new opportunities if we are able to not get so personally involved or perhaps not allow ourselves to take what is being said personally. God is able to cause all things to work together for the good of everyone involved.

Chapter 7

DEALING WITH WORKPLACE ANGER

NO ONE IS SURPRISED WHEN A STORY ON THE NEWS SHOWS AN EMPLOYEE that has gone into their work environment and has gunned down several of their fellow employees, whether they were known to him or not. The question that always seems to be asked, but is never really answered with a tremendous amount of detail, is why? In many of these tragic situations, the employee was angry with another employee or with management. Several of these criminal incidents are often the results of some kind of conflict or disagreement between co-workers.

As I am writing this chapter, a news flash just appeared on the television showing a man in Aurora, Illinois has just gone into a manufacturing plant and gunned down 5 co-workers, injured 5 police officers and has injured several other people as well. Apparently, he was going to be fired for a reason that has not been released to the public. He apparently intended on getting revenge by taking the lives of individuals in the human resource department. According to the report, he worked at the plant for 15 years. Obviously he had violated policy or had failed to meet the expectations of management. To him, however, he didn't deserve to get fired, and someone was going to pay. These type of situations, which have happened all too frequently in the past few years, stem from uncontrolled anger that is deep within those who commit such diabolical acts. When a person stays within themselves and does not know how to manage the thinking that begins to bubble up into the emotion of anger, they are now in danger of committing an act that will bring destruction to many people. This type of behavior, of course, is the extreme of what can happen.

When we consider anger in the workplace, it truly can lead to scary scenarios. People who get upset or who are prone to being quick-tempered are easily triggered if there is something that takes place that they don't like or that offends them. Quick-tempered individuals are capable of allowing their emotion of anger to dictate their action. In the case of the mass shooting with the man in Aurora, Illinois with his co-workers, that is apparently what happened. The emotion of anger overruled his rational thought process. It is impossible to know what event is going to cause people to "go off." I would say the closest way of knowing if a person has a potential for violence is to observe their pattern of behavior. Does the behavior that is currently being exhibited appear to escalate or get more aggressive over time? Does the person show signs of frustration on a regular basis or display anger when under pressure? Do they show any signs of depression or have they been isolating themselves from other people?

The employee who shot his co-workers should not have had a gun legally, as he also had a criminal record. Somehow he fell through the cracks when it came to the security check. This should never happen, yet it does. Can we be honest for a minute? Contrary to many people who believe in the over- regulation of guns, gun control is not really the issue. Gun control can only do so much. When we consider how guns can be gotten on the black market or the street, we can then come to the conclusion that if a person is angry enough to consider shooting those who they feel have offended them, they will find a way to get a gun illegally. The human heart is the culprit. The human heart is subjected to evil constantly and, in some instances, some will surrender and give in to the evil. Jeremiah 17:9 lets us know that "the heart is deceitful and desperately wicked." These words come straight out of Scripture. Unfortunately many people have turned their minds and their hearts away from God's Word. If humankind is deceived, they are deceived in many areas of their lives, and a major area is one that deals with their anger. James says it like this in Chapter 4:1-3. "What causes fights and quarrels among you? Don't they come from your desires that battle within you? You want something but don't get it. You kill and covet, but you cannot have what you want. You quarrel and fight. You do not have, because you do not ask God. When you ask, you do not receive, because you ask with wrong motives, that you may spend what you get on your pleasures."

The quarrels or conflicts that arise come about because of what a person doesn't get. For example: I believe that I deserve a pay raise. I don't get it, so now I am angry. I believe that I was treated unfairly, unjustly, or inappropriately, but no one saw it the way that I did. Another example might be: I believe that I am now being fired without just cause. I am now angry, or I tried to give my supervisor positive feedback on how to do something better, but it is not received the way I believed it should have been. I am now angry. Other examples might include having a complaint about another employee that falls on deaf ears, or being up for a promotion and feeling you're the best person for the position but not getting it. All these scenarios can happen in the workplace and can easily cause someone to feel offended and justified in becoming angry. Notice what I didn't say? I didn't say that you *shouldn't* be angry. Most of the aforementioned situations are plausible and, to some degree, justifiable. One's anger can be based on injustice and, if injustice is present, the anger is justified. The key factor is how does one use the anger to see some kind of result that is positive. Most individuals will not look at their anger from this perspective. However, looking at the situation in this way creates a way to take the anger and use it as fuel for change, whether it be change on a personal level, change regarding a co-worker or possibly a change in policy. Allow the anger to precipitate change, not destruction.

When looking at the man who just committed this despicable mass shooting, unfortunately, we will not be able to know why he felt he needed to kill people because he himself was killed in a gun fight with the police. But look at the destruction that has come about because of his anger over losing his job; look at the families who were affected. There are now wives with no husbands, kids with no fathers, mothers experiencing a loss of their children. Then there are the injured police officers who have to deal with recovery and who possibly could have lost their lives. Then there is the family of the man who committed the act. It doesn't make any sense that a person should feel justified in committing such violence. It is, without a doubt, evil. From a spiritual perspective, there is one person who gets joy out of this kind of destruction of life, that being Satan. This is what Satan does; if he can get people to make decisions in their anger, destruction will be the next result.

John 10:10 says, "10 The thief comes only to steal and kill and destroy; I [Jesus] have come that they may have life, and have it to the full." This verse indicates that Satan purposely goes around to steal, kill and destroy. He steals hearts, lives, dreams, and all those things that God desires us to have. He kills relationships, lives, dreams, and ministries, those things that are precious to God and to us. Satan is about hurt, harm and pain. I hope that you can see now that if he can keep you angry, something in your life, as well as the lives of others, can be stolen, killed or destroyed. Learning to control anger, in general and not just in the workplace is a tremendous preventative measure that can protect us wherever we are because we never know what is going to happen next.

A necessary key to effectively handling anger in the workplace is knowing if the work environment is actually producing the anger. It was stated earlier that a person who has anger issues has a problem with recognizing the anger in himself/herself. We must realize and accept the fact that one person doesn't make another person angry. A person who is angry *reacts* with the emotion of anger and, when coupled with other emotions, results in quiet or demonstrative destructive and explosive behavior. An employee must identify whether the anger is being projected on another employee or is revealing itself through how the person feels toward himself/herself. The anger can still be projected onto someone else even though the person is angry at himself/herself. Anger that is projected by a person onto someone else makes the person projecting the anger feel justified. In fact, the employee who is angry will create a reason why they are angry at the other employee(s) even if they didn't do anything to that person.

An example of anger projection occurred one time when I was manager at the Horticulture Center. An employee was extremely upset at me because of how I had changed something around. He never told me that he was upset because he was the type of person who exhibited passive-aggressive behavior. Their anger permeated their behavior in subtle ways in order to get back at me. Even though the person was mad with me, technically he was mad at himself because he didn't know how to deal with it differently. Have you ever come across those individuals who know that you are right about things, but they won't accept it because they dislike you? I would even say that there was some displacement occurring as well – that is, putting something on me that actually should have been put on someone else. We will talk about this shortly.

Over the past few weeks, Jussie Smolett has been in the news claiming that he was attacked on a street of Chicago at 2 AM in the morning by two men who yelled racial and homophobic slurs at him, poured some kind of liquid on him, and put a noose around his neck. After several days, the police discovered that the entire thing was staged by him. His lawyers, as well as Smolett himself, are still insisting that it wasn't his fault and that he is innocent. He has not totally owned up to what he is allegedly accused of. The entire incident appears to have been staged because he was thinking totally about himself and wasn't considering the impact of his actions on others. When he was interviewed by Robin Roberts on "Good Morning, America," he was angry and was very accusatory toward individuals who supported the President. He had already been extremely vocal about the President and the conservatives who supported him. He took what was a symbol of history, coupled it with his identification of being black and gay, and was using the media to promote personal gain. His stunt fed into the anger and emotion of what had already been emoting from the political arena for the past couple of years. His stunt fed into the emotional environment and was supported by the media. He attempted and wanted to take advantage of the environment in order to falsely accuse those who had nothing to do with the incident.

I use the above situation to point out how anger can make a person do things that are destructive to themselves and others. Projection of anger can be placed on people who have nothing to do with why a person is angry in any number of situations. I believe this takes place in the workplace on a regular basis. Think about the anger that Smolett helped to produce in his co-workers on the set of Empire, the TV series in which he was a cast member. It appears that the stunt was to enable him to get more money... but I missed understanding something here: How does staging a hoax get you more money at your job? Then he claims that he is innocent. When we look at the Scripture we are able to see that Jesus and Paul were falsely accused of insurrection. They both ended up dying for something that they never did. Yet, the ones who were accusing them of what they weren't doing were the ones actually guilty of insurrection themselves. This goes to show you that nothing has changed and every generation of people is the same in this respect.

Have you ever thought about how people get angry when they actually have other feelings that are present? In many situations, people use anger when they cannot properly handle their other emotions. For example, if someone has a poor self-image, they can get angry at a comment that wasn't directed toward them, but because of where they are mentally, the tendency is for them to search the environment to justify their anger, all while supporting their poor self-image. When in the workplace, this person will be on edge mostly all the time due to their negative view of themselves.

As believers, we are to be slow to anger and this principle is to be applied in every possible situation. Being slow to anger means that we are in a posture of not reacting quickly when things happen unexpectedly. When anger is lurking, we should do something about it before it is expressed in a sinful way. Anger is not the problem; it is what is *done* with the anger. If anger is used to bring about change, then it becomes positive.

At this juncture, I would like to bring in another thought process. In the world of psychotherapy, there is a word that is used known as transference, which I mentioned earlier. Transference occurs when a person places expectations, needs, beliefs, attitudes, feelings, fantasies, etc., on others that actually belong to their parents, siblings, friends, significant others, etc. When one transfers characteristics to individuals that aren't really the problem, what appears to be true for the projecting person, in reality is an illusion; it is not real. The person is now taking their emotions out on the wrong people. Another term that is used in psychoanalytical circles is the word projection, which we also talked about earlier. This occurs when a person projects on to another person those feelings, expectations, etc. that are actually what is in him/her. The person is in a state of denial, not believing that he/she have an issue with himself/herself. They are sold on the fact that it is the *other* person who is the problem. A good example of this is complaining about a person being a control freak when, in reality, the person complaining is the control freak. I might as well mention one more word, which is displacement. Displacement occurs when a person is angry or upset with one person and then places it on another person, as if that second were the one who had created the anger in them. An example of this might be: I experienced a bad day at baseball practice. I was extremely upset with Bob who teased me the entire practice. I then came home and begin to take it out on my little brother, but I am angry at the wrong person. Think: if a person is experiencing one, two or all three of these psycho-analytical characteristics, how easy it would be for them to blow up at work or at home. The possibility exists that they could lose it at any given time anywhere.

People who allow their past to invade their present this way on a regular basis will be subject to living in a state of delusion most of their lives unless they get counseling to begin the process of change. People who transfer are constantly living in the past by allowing their past to control their present, constantly yielding to those voices or people in their past. It doesn't matter how far or how close the past might be for them; it could have been yesterday. The past prevents a person from a successful future because of the presence of the past that is being engaged by the person. These psychological conditions, I am sure, are producing a great deal of the anger in the workplace. By exercising one or more of these practices, a person is trying to protect their bodies and their minds from stress but, as a direct result, miserably failing at it.

A healthy person will not use these practices and will stay in reality. Staying in reality is being able to look back at the past or look at oneself honestly and accept what truly is. In John 8:32, John lets us know that Jesus was in a conversation with the Pharisees. Jesus makes a statement that is profound, when you think about it, and is one of those gems that can have a major impact on how we live, if we allow it to do so. Jesus lets us know the truth, in the context of living out our faith, will set us free. Truth, especially in regards to the innermost parts of ourselves, can only be realized in the context of faith in Christ. God's truth tears apart our tendency of wanting to blame others for where we are and why we behave the way we do. Truth causes us to look square in the eye some of the lies that we have been living, most likely, for many years. Anger helps to keep the lies in tact, when you really think about it, because anger can help to cover and protect us from getting to what is really wrong with us. If the lies are never exposed so that they might be eradicated from our minds, how does one move forward? When we are able to look upon our past as a witness, without adding anything to it, it stands for itself and serves as a reference. When we get involved with our past as a participant, we have then allowed our past to have say-so in our present which will impact our future. What a difference in the workplace when our perspective lines up with the gospel, which is then implemented in our lives! Instead of shooting people in the workplace, we can go in and ask what we can do next time that would help us keep our job. Accepting the firing graciously, knowing that we brought it on ourselves, would speak volumes to the employer. Jesus will have us go counterculture with our responses. What a testimony for Him who is our Savior!

Chapter 8

LEADERSHIP HAPPENS WHETHER YOU WANT IT TO OR NOT

I LOVE SPORTS; MOST MEN DO. IT DOESN'T MATTER WHAT SPORT IT IS that I am watching – football, baseball, basketball, or hockey – I am going to be into the game. It is great when one team wins and not so great when the other team loses. It is the competitive nature of the teams that are playing that make the games enjoyable. Usually there is one person, and in many instances, several individuals on the team who are leaders. Some of these leaders have a natural ability to emerge as such because it is in them. Others have matured over the years and because of their experience became leaders in the clubhouse or locker room. Some are appointed leaders by their teammates or by the coaches. It is commonplace for most sports teams to have leaders that are players who help to speak into the younger players' lives, especially if there are issues that are affecting their "rookie" performance.

When we see how a child attach themselves to a certain player, that player becomes a role model to that child whether the player is aware of it or not, or whether the player wants to be a role or not.

It just happens unknowingly. When a child is focused on a particular player exclusively, that player represents something in that child's life that most likely is not being fulfilled by those close to them. There is a vicarious relationship formed by the child. The child watches everything that player does, on the court and off the court, on the field or off the field, on the ice or off the ice. With social media, sources such as YouTube, Facebook, Twitter, and Instagram, it is pretty easy to follow someone we really don't know. That sports player for that child is capable of impacting a child's life by merely being present on social media. The player, behavior-wise, could be a negative influence, and could very well be acting like themselves. Being themselves could be negative, if the player tends not to care or be concerned about how they behave during the game or during their off time. What emerges out of this type of situation still represents leadership for that child, though the player is not even aware on a personal level that he or she is even having any kind of influence.

Several years ago when Charles Barkley was playing basketball, someone had asked him what he thought about himself when it came to being a role model for young children. Charles said "It isn't my job to be a role model." I believe he then said that that was not what he was trying to be. Even though Charles didn't purposely want to be a role model, kids were looking at him as one, merely by his being an elite sports figure. If one person is watching me as a player, observing what I do and how I do it, and then they do it I, without any intent and purpose, have become a leader to that person. There are many circumstances in which people play roles where they don't see themselves as leaders, but the function that they are performing puts them into the role of a leader. For example, consider a stay-at-home mother. She might not look at taking care of children as being a leader, but isn't that what she is doing every day? She is watching over, giving direction to, and being an example for her children; she is providing leadership. By the way, I do understand that in today's culture that there are stay-at-home dads. The same would apply with them as well with regards to their being a leader for their children. Let me add this, however: Fathers, whether they are at home watching their children or not, have been given the responsibility by God to be the leader of their families. The husband is responsible for every member of the family and is intentionally given the position of leadership by God Himself. When we see individuals who are being mentored by someone in a specific area or in general, that mentor is also being a leader. When a child is making decisions for the other children in the group at school during recess, they are being a leader. When an employee who has been on a job for several years and is asked to train a new employee they, in essence, have stepped into the role as a leader. Even in the animal kingdom, leaders emerge out of the pack due to survival of the fittest. What about the mother duck who is leading a flock of her ducklings; isn't that also a display of leadership? Leadership is all around us, whether we intentionally are cognizant of it or not.

So, exactly what is the real definition of leadership? According to one definition, leadership is "the action of leading people or an organization" (Source: Wikipedia.) I recall hearing a definition years ago that leadership is "taking people where they won't go on their own." Leadership, when you truly think about it, is a concept and can be defined differently depending on what is needed. For some, leadership is motivation; for others, it could equal results, and for still others, it's inspiration. Is leadership just applied to groups, even though the definition seems to imply a group in its wording? Consider some of the synonyms for leadership: guidance, direction, authority, management, supervision, influence, and initiative. When considering these words, I believe it is safe to say that leadership can apply to two people who are involved in a relationship. When we consider the Scripture, we see that God placed the man in the position of leader over his family. At the establishment of the first family, only Adam and Eve were present. God had to make someone responsible for overseeing the family structure, and that was Adam. It wasn't a question of the man being physically stronger or more intelligent. God appointed the man the position because God was the one who was calling the shots. He was the Creator and established things the way that He wanted. Headship was God-ordained and cannot be overturned by any human.

When we now look in the workplace, leadership can be very complex. What makes me say that? There are a combination of factors. There are those individuals who have become supervisors, or managers or any other type of upper management person through taking a test, usually in government settings. These individuals are in the job because they were good test takers, not necessarily because they were good leaders. Some of the supervisors whom I experienced over the years as a government employee working with other city agencies, or in the context of the church, have exhibited terrible people skills and end up staying in these positions for years. I would say that 75% of any supervisory position requires people skills. In jobs where there were appointments, the supervision could be just as bad or even worse when it came to people skills as well as communication skills. This could be due to nepotism or the advocating of one person over the other, not because of their ability, but just being favored. It has been my experience to have those who weren't in positions with the title of supervisor to be more helpful than those who were in those titled positions. Co-workers come to them because of their knowledge of the job and their people skills. On the other hand, there are those who have the ability to stir things up in the workplace and instigating circumstances in order to create drama. They are leaders, due to their influence on others, but in a negative way that brings about dysfunction. Then there are those who are natural followers and will move whatever direction seems right or beneficial at the time. Within this group of followers, who don't say much, a sub-culture can emerge where there is a leader among them that can have influence on the other followers. If one of their self-appointed leaders does not particularly like something, they might be able to influence the others not to like it also. Then there are those who will take up criticism for another person. In taking their criticism, they begin to speak up for the person and now become their spokes-person. This is also a type of leadership.

The kind of supervisor we would have in the workplace would determine how much work would get done. It could range from very little to a great deal, when it came to what actually got done. If no one followed up to check what was completed, the desired quality or quantity of work might not be accomplished. If there are no measures in place to make sure the work is completed, that it is done properly and done well, then does leadership actually occur? Look at the definition again: "taking people where they would not go on their own." This process can occur through example with or without direct personal involvement. So if we were to look at several job situations, we can honestly conclude that there are many individuals who are given leadership positions, but they aren't leaders because they are not taking people anywhere. They themselves need close supervision. There are employees who go and do what they want and actually can get away with doing the bare minimum. Unfortunately, a culture or environment can be created over years that will lend itself to extremely low employee productivity. This kind of culture creates an environment that produces a proliferation of negative, unproductive attitudes among those who come in later, that were present among those who were there in the past. I have seen this happen in government or public employment settings, and would venture it happens in many other places. With environments like what was described above, or if it would be the "perfect" workplace environment, what should leadership look like with a believer in Jesus?

I am going to point to a very interesting verse of Scripture in Acts Chapter I. Jesus was resurrected and had appeared to people over a period of 40 days, speaking about the kingdom of God. During one period of time, as he was eating with his disciples, he gave them this word that would impact their lives in Acts 1:8.

"But you will receive power when the Holy Spirit comes on you; and you will be my witnesses in Jerusalem, and in all Judea and Samaria, and to the ends of the earth."

This verse would not only apply to the disciples and other followers of Christ who were present when He made the statement, but would also be applicable to any disciple or follower of Christ thereafter. If you are a believer in Jesus, and genuinely living for Him, then this verse applies to your life as well. So the believer in Jesus had been given the Holy Spirit, which would provide power in their lives to be able to live and love like Jesus. The power that we have been given enables us to be witnesses for Jesus anywhere and everywhere, just like the disciples back then. Being a witness with the power of Jesus is a lifestyle that does not change or get lost when we are in the workplace, or whether outside or inside a church building.

The question to be asked is: How does being a witness for Jesus equate or evolve into being a leader? As a witness for Jesus, we are literally showing individuals an alternative lifestyle that pleases God, as well as what God desires every person to have. Every believer is called by God to be an ambassador of the kingdom of God (Romans 5:20). Specifically, we are ambassadors of Christ who minister reconciliation. The believer then has been given the Holy Spirit and power to be witnesses for the purpose of reconciling those who don't know Jesus back to God. This example occurs through our example with our lives and our mouths. Let's bring in our leadership definition along with what Christ has made us become. We now are helping people to go where they are not going on their own in the workplace. For the believer, that would include: to endeavor to be the best worker they can be and not to get angry or lose control; not to participate in certain events or gatherings that might be questionable; not to complain about things that might be wrong even when others are complaining; to love people when they are unlovable; to pray for those who are mistreating you; to be willing to tell people the truth when no one else will; to have the willingness to be vulnerable when necessary; as a supervisor, not to be afraid to be merciful toward co-workers and to be meek, which is to have power that is under control.

When at work, believers who understand Scripture do not become somebody different than what they are outside of work. We don't put on or put off who we are like a T-shirt being pulled over our head. We merely apply the same biblical principles that we need to apply at home, in our neighborhood, or anywhere else. In fact, the workplace is training ground for us to grow in our faith. Work tends to be the place where we are challenged to be authentic. We are tested in the workplace because there are so many different types of people that make us uncomfortable and we really don't want to be bothered with them or even interact with them. It is the workplace where God wants us to display the power of the Holy Spirit that overcomes all the obstacles that would be hard for us in our humanness, but is no problem for the fruit of the Spirit that comes from the Lord (Gal. 5:22). When we step aside and allow the Holy Spirit to do His work, we have become a leader through being an example of what it is like to be a witness for Jesus. Leadership, from God's perspective, evolves out of brokenness. As a person rises out of their pain and hurt, as well as their weaknesses, God shines through them more and more. In the midst of our pains and hurts in the workplace, God still gives us the ability to be a witness. His desire is for us to lead in godliness and we are able to do that through the power of the Holy Spirit.

I have been a manager in municipal government and I have been an administrator and Christian educator in the church world. It really doesn't matter which world you work in because the people, whether believers or not, go through the same issues. In both sce-narios, there was leadership training for the purpose of becoming a better leader. I learned a lot from the training in both settings; to be honest, both were similar in content. Most all leadership training focuses on becoming successful at leading. When looking at what Jesus said in Acts 1:8, where do we find leadership training, the training that is received is through the Holy Spirit, who gives power to do what is necessary to be witnesses. We do know that the 12 apostles walked with Jesus and were involved in being mentored by the Greatest Teacher ever – Jesus. The point I want to make is that the leadership that we get from human training is different than what God has called us to be as witnesses for Him. Living a life before people that exhibits who He is, is the greatest leadership that one can experience. Paul, when he writes to Timothy in II Timothy 4:7 says to him " I have kept the faith." In context, the faith is like a trust that a person has for someone. It is an arrangement whereby a person holds property as its nominal owner for the good or more beneficiaries. The Lord had entrusted Paul with the "faith." So what Paul is saying is that he kept the terms of the contract; he had managed and looked after the trust faithfully and well. Through all the suffering, all the trials, all the evil accusations that he faced, he never gave up or threw away the trust (faith) that was given to him to hold. Paul was able to never give up his faith no matter what situation he faced. Paul was born in sin like we are, yet he experienced Jesus. If Paul was able to endure all that he did without wavering from faith, why can't we do it in the workplace? We have the power living in us to be the witnesses that the world definitely needs to see and experience.

Chapter 9

IT'S ALL IN THE MIND

A FEW YEARS AGO, DURING THE 2016 FOOTBALL SEASON, NELSON AGHOLOR, a wide receiver for the Philadelphia Eagles, had a very difficult year. He was the 20th overall pick in the 2015 draft and was expected to be a premier wide receiver in the league. Unfortunately, things did not go very well for him in the 2016 season. Because he was a 1st round draft pick, it was expected that he would do great things and would be a major part of the Eagles receiving corp. The season for him was an absolute bust. Every game it seemed as if he would drop more and more balls that were thrown directly to him. He wasn't hanging onto anything. It was as if he had oil on his hands which caused him to drop the ball almost every time it came his direction. Balls that were in his hands, he seemed not to hold on to. It truly was a tough thing to watch him every single game as ball after ball would fall to the ground. It was quite obvious that mentally he was struggling and had lost all his confidence. Some wondered if he would ever be able to come back or recover from such a horrible season.

When we look at individuals who play sports at such a high level – a professional level – we must understand the mental aspect that is part of the game. For Nelson, mentally he must have been in a very bad place, knowing what the expectation was for him when he was drafted. The expectation that is placed on a first-round draft pick is pressure-filled. The mental and productivity aspects of these players' capacities, no matter what sport, must be of great significance as a professional. The toughness that is needed game after game in order to maintain a winning record is an amazing feat. When a team is winning, it is easy to have a positive, confident attitude. But what about when the team loses regularly? How can you maintain the same attitude as you do when the team is winning? You even see the difference when a team has "home advantage." There is something about the setting and the environment of knowing that there is a crowd behind you, rooting for you to perform well. However, in Nelson's case that year, it didn't matter that the crowd was there. In fact, it probably made it harder because of their expectations not being fulfilled in terms of his ability to catch the balls thrown to him.

Our sports analogy regarding the importance of mindset not only applies to sports, of course, but to work in general. Some might consider those who play sports not being at an actual job. However, it is a job in that the players make millions and millions of dollars doing. There are expectations and performance quotas that are expected to be met. Isn't this the same criteria that is part of most work environments? So mindset is a major aspect for these players; the mind is where everything is being processed. The way that a person wakes up in the morning and comes to work can be affected by what has taken place at home the night before, if not handled appropriately. The mind, of course, is where thinking is carried out. How one thinks about circumstances that occur in the present or in the past can impact attitude, which will then impact how one will treat people in the workplace upon their arrival. Those individuals who have trained their minds to be disciplined in regard to external circumstances are better able to maintain a proper sense of self and maintain a level of normalcy when at work. Those who aren't disciplined in this way will allow their thinking to have an impact on their work performance and possibly their interaction with co-workers.

As believers in Christ, the Bible gives us a great deal of insight regarding our mindset. One of the verses that has an immediate impact can be found in Philippians 2:5 where Paul writes "Let this mind be in you which was also in Christ Jesus." In order to know what Paul is referring to, one must read the verses before and after to verse 5. Having a mind like Christ means having a love for others that puts other individuals first, a humility that places oneself last. It means having a willingness to look at the person as being better than yourself, and a mind that is willing to be on the same page as God. Additionally, there must also be a willingness to look out for the other person's best interest. As you can see, taking on the mind of Christ is not that easy, especially in the workplace. If we dig a little deeper in the verse, we are able to see that Jesus voluntarily did what He did – that is, leaving heaven to come to earth – because of a deep love that He had for all of us. Notice something: we are able to fulfill His joy by being like-minded. Allowing His mind to dominate our mind and allowing the thinking that emanates from His mind to our mind will enable us to then put into practice whatever His mind is directing us to do. This process is not robotic, but voluntary. We give up what we want to do in order to submit to what He wants us to do. This is out of an act of obedience. What He wants will come out of His mind and, as we allow it to permeate into ours, obedience evolves out of it. This is the process of surrender. God's mind is pure, is all love and is always in a place of humility.

Jesus left heaven and humbled Himself in order to submit Himself to His creation as well as the sovereignty of the Father, even unto death. He shows us how to live in humility and how to consider others first; He put us first over Himself. Yet most will find it difficult to practice this principle at home as well as at work. Yes, I know He is God, but He was walking as a man who was in flesh at this point in time. Paul was not a God-man, yet we see how his mind is yielded to the mind of Christ. Paul tells us in Romans 12:1 that we must be transformed by the renewing of our minds; renewing our minds begins when we align our minds with Christ. Our minds need to be renewed when it comes to work. In Chapter One, we talked about where work came from and why it existed, so we can start there. Seeing that work is directly tied into our relationship with God is the starting point.

When I started my job as a manager, I had a desire to be a different type of manager. I truly wanted to be a servant leader; that was my desire when I began. Was I successful in doing that? I hope that I was, but I am sure that most of my co-workers didn't think so. However, I knew what my motives were. My mindset, by having a desire to be a servant leader, was one that aligned with the Scripture. This mindset was not quite that of some in management, I hope you know that. There were some practices that I did not desire to be part of my management style because of my faith. What were some of those things, you might ask? I found it commonplace for many managers to curse at their co-workers. I never did that. There were some managers who were extremely friendly with many of their employees. There were a few with whom I became friendly, but I wasn't chummy-chummy with most. The problem that can rear its head in many of these situations is the failure to discipline when necessary. When friends with co-workers who are subordinates, there will be the expectation among some of those co-workers that they can get away with things. Now you see where mindset comes into the picture. A distorted mindset can be found on both sides because expectations will naturally be birthed out of closeness. These expectations can be unspoken, however, and there is a difference between extending grace to an employee after you warned them as opposed to not saying a word to them and letting the behavior continue. Extending grace and mercy comes out of the compassion that exists because of the presence of God. However, discipline should be administered if the behavior doesn't change.

Having the mindset of Christ on the job, when it comes to most employees, will not be understood. It doesn't matter if co-workers understand what you are doing or not. Biblical principles aren't being applied in order to get recognition, but to bring glory to God. The mindset of a believer must be one of willingness, not desiring anything in return. In fact, we might get something worse coming back at us. Knowing that God is the one who has provided for our employment, as well as enabled us to wake up to go to work each and every day, should give us a grateful heart. An attitude of gratitude should envelop our hearts and our minds. After the "honeymoon" at our jobs, which could last 1 to 5 years, many will get discouraged; this appears to be normal. It is during times like these, when we have become disheartened with our type of employment, that our minds must be renewed. In this context, I would like to share an experience with you.

It was in the mid-ninety's when I was a the Horticulture Center. I was at a point in my life where I wanted to leave the job; I felt that I wasn't where I needed to be job-wise. I really felt that I wasn't having an impact on people the way that I should and that God wanted me in full-time ministry; I was truly struggling. I would pester my wife, Beverly, all the time about wanting to leave it. One weekend, I attended the PenDel Arborist Conference which took place in Lancaster. I would attend every year because I needed CEU's (Continuing Education Units) in order to maintain my Certified Arborist license. Instead of staying at the hotel where the conference was held, I would stay with a pastor friend of mine and his wife; they lived in Ephrata, PA. I had been staying with them for several years prior during the week of the conference, but this particular year would turn out to be truly meaningful. He had become a great friend and I was able to talk to him about what I had been dealing with.

What changed for me that February evening as we sat and talked and watched the Super Bowl was my mindset. I was able to have a renewed mind because someone spoke truth into my situation – not just truth that emanates from the mind of a man, but God's truth that emanates from the mind of God. God's truth is able to alter the faulty thinking that invades our minds on occasion. It is crucial to have people in our lives that can challenge our thinking when we sink to levels that aren't normal for us. My friend's words caused me to look at what I was thinking about myself at the time. I was able to stay on the job that I wanted to leave for another decade and a half, not because I all of a sudden loved it, but because I was able to see it from a perspective that was greater than mine. I came to understand that what I was doing was having an impact for the kingdom of God, even though I didn't think so.

Going to a job every day, involved with the same people and doing the same thing for many years, can be a daunting task. Some people do what they do because that's all they can do. The mindset is what can be the difference in how the job is approached. When one has a mindset that is shaped by Christ, and can see what they do as vital to the kingdom, it brings glory to God and that is the greater calling. Your mindset when attached to a higher purpose can alter how you view what you do. Think again about how Jesus left heaven to come to earth. Couldn't He have found another way? Not really! Why? Because of who He is; He took the road that shows humility. What should make us different is the humility that we should be exhibiting, even in the midst of us not liking what we do. Jesus didn't come to make us happy, but to make us holy. We have the opportunity of showing that holiness through our mindset, which is our attitude.

The Philadelphia 76er's are having a pretty decent year and it looks like they are headed to the playoffs. What is interesting is that they have a point guard that is afraid to shoot the ball more than 10 to 12 feet from the basket. A point guard should have a jump shot. After 2 years of playing professional basketball, the player hardly wants to attempt to shoot a jumper. Is it mindset? I would say yes, most likely. In order for him to change the mindset, there might be two things involved; one is mental and the other is physical. He probably needs to see a sports psychologist who can help his mental state, as well as obtain a shooting coach who can help him develop his jump shot. He can receive both, but in order to see results, he must implement what he learns from both. The psychologist will help him to focus and to gain confidence and security, while the shooting coach will help him with technique and form. As they work in tandem, results can be realized over time.

These same principles apply to our workplace. God provides us with that which comes from Him as our Counselor and the coaches in our lives are those we glean wisdom from as well as the people we do life with. Your mindset changes through the implementation of both of these factors working in tandem with each other. Thomas, one of the disciples in John 20 didn't believe Jesus had resurrected from the grave. He emphatically said out loud among the other disciples that unless he can touch the place where Jesus was wounded, he would not believe. Well, guess what? Jesus allowed him to do the very thing he had requested. Upon his touching Jesus, he declared, "My Lord, My God!" Within a few seconds there was a change in mindset; he went from unbelief to belief, from skeptic to believer, from doubt to assurance. Jesus doesn't have a problem with unbelief; He wants us to be open to believe. He was able to impact Thomas by granting his request to touch Him. What are we asking Jesus to do in regard to our mindset at our jobs? Have we asked Him to do things that aren't within our power to change? Do we desire Him to do something through us that is greater? Are we just dying on the vine at work or are we recognizing that by us being part of the vine, Jesus is able to produce fruit through us at our jobs? Where is it that you need to touch Jesus, so that Jesus can grant your request?

Living out the gospel at work will be seen through our attitudes as believers. From the janitor to the executive, God wants us to exemplify Jesus. What a great opportunity to put God on display! Are we willing to yield who we are at work to Him? If the answer is yes, that means that there will be a radical difference in how you approach co-workers. You will see them as neighbors to be loved, as opposed to just people that you work with. Remember Nelson Agholor and that terrible year he had in 2016? Apparently, he went to see a sports psychologist and worked hard during the off season in 2017. In the training camp of 2017, a new Nelson was present. He was catching everything that came his way. He went from "Mr. Unreliable" to "Mr. Reliable" in 2017. He was instrumental in helping the Eagles win the Super Bowl that year because he made some key catches in that game. What made the difference in Nelson from 2016 to 2017? It was mindset. He showed up at camp with confidence and a mindset that showed he was able to be trusted when the ball was thrown in his direction. What a difference a year makes! Isn't it Nelson's job to have done what he needed to do to be the best at what he does at work, which is playing football? Ben Simmons, whom I was referring to earlier, is the point guard that can't shoot jumpers. But it is his job to learn to shoot them; he is getting paid to perform. If he is weak in an area, he should be willing to do whatever is necessary to improve. That is what separates the good players from the great players. No matter how good a player might be, even if they are a natural at what they do, good players become great because of their desire to keep getting better at what they do. It should be our endeavor to be all that Jesus wants us to be at our jobs and it begins with mindset. A renewed mind will bring about new possibilities as well as the potential to impact co-workers for Christ. Isn't that our real job? That is what separates the good and the great, at least from God's perspective.

Chapter 10

STRESSED, FOR WHAT?

HAVE YOU EVER ASKED THE QUESTION, WHAT IS THE MOST STRESSFUL JOB in America? Most would think to say that it would be President of the United States, a doctor, or a CEO of a big corporation. I most certainly consider occupations such as those to be at the top of my list. Most people think that the jobs that they do every day are stressful, but some may be more entitled to complain than others. There was a survey conducted in 2018 by Career Cast, an organization that tracks such data. They found that 78% of people feel unduly stressed in the workplace. Most rated their stress on the job at a 7 or higher on a 10-point scale. Two years ago, the same survey was administered and it was found to be 69%. That is an increase of 9% over the two year period.

What was it that was stressing all these people out in the workplace? The answer is workers having to deal with frequent hard deadlines. Over 35% of the people surveyed agreed on that point; the exact number was 38%. Growth potential and interacting with the public tied for 2nd place, with 14% of people articulating that these two (2) things mentioned being the top culprits. According to an analysis at Career Cast, if you were to mix in a danger component, it would create the perfect storm.

Career Cast evaluated 201 occupations on 11 different factors, which were

1. Travel demands
2. Environmental conditions
3. Physical demands
4. Deadlines
5. Interacting with the public
6. Working in the public eye
7. Growth potential
8. Completions in the field
9. Hazards encountered on a regular basis
10. Responsibility for the safety of others
11. Potential for harm/or death

Source (www.careercast.com/2018)

Career Cast also found that the following 10 jobs were the most stressful in the United States:

Occupation Annual	Median Salary
1. Enlisted Military Personnel	$26,802
2. Firefighter	$49,080
3. Airplane Pilot	$111,930
4. Police Officer	$62,050
5. Broadcaster	$62,910

6.	Event Coordinator	$48,290
7.	News Reporter	$39,370
8.	Public Relations Executive	$111,280
9.	Senior Corporate Executive	$104,700
10.	Taxi Driver	$24,880

Source (www.careercast.com/2018)

Wow! The most stressful job in the United States pays second to the least amount of money to those who perform it. Since we are now able to see who actually has the most stressful jobs, according to research, let's look at the least stressful jobs in the United States. The occupations below all scored at the very bottom of Career Cast's rankings of the most stressful jobs in America. Remember, their scores were based on those 11 different factors.

Occupation	Annual Median Salary
1. Diagnostic Medical Sonographer	$71,410
These healthcare workers create images of the body's organs and tissues. These are known as sonograms or ultra sounds	
2. Compliance Officer	$67,870
Ensure that a company follows regulatory requirements in their own internal polices	
3. Hair Stylist	$25,850
Make people look good by styling their hair	
4. Audiologist	$75,920
Healthcare workers who diagnose and	

treat patient's hearing issues, balance and
other related problems like tinnitus

5. University Professor $76,000
Teaching students and conducting research,
writing books and scholarly papers

6. Medical Record Technician $67,080
Healthcare who workers ensure patient
health information is accurate and secure

7. Jeweler $37,960
Designing, appraising, repairing
and selling jewelry

8. Operations Research Analyst $61,390
Workers using advanced mathematical
and analytical methods to help businesses
solve problems

9. Pharmacy technician $31,750
Healthcare workers who dispense
prescription medication to customers

10. Massage Therapist $39,990
Workers relax and treat clients by
manipulating the muscles and soft tissues
of the body to relieve pain and stress

Source (www.careercast.com/2018)

The above jobs, as mentioned, were at the low end of the stress scale. We can say that all the other jobs, at least using the jobs we just mentioned, fall between the most stressful and the least stressful jobs. I would like to mention the most stress-free job in history, at least from my point of view, and that is the job done by Vanna White on Wheel of Fortune. She has been at this job since 1982. That is over 35 years. What is her job? Turning letters. Talk about stress free! Her salary is $4 million per year, and she works only 4 days a month. Source (www.Goodhousekeeping.com.) That is what I would call a dream job!

But what is stress anyway? It is a state of mental or emotional strain or tension resulting from adverse or very demanding circumstances. Another definition is something that causes strong feelings of worry or anxiety. Looking at stress from a psychological perspective, the definition includes the fact that stress can affect people of all ages, genders and circumstances and can lead to both physical and psychological health issues. By definition, stress is any uncomfortable emotional experience accompanied by predictable biochemical, physiological and behavioral changes.

Source – www.google.com.

Maybe we need to reconsider how we think about stress. The definition reveals that there is a strain in the emotional as well as the mental areas of our lives. What if whatever we are going through was able to be handled without the strain? Is it possible to handle very difficult – or what we perceive to be difficult – issues in our lives? I believe the Bible lets us know that it *is* possible. However, in order to experience the reality of not having the strain – or at least a minimized level of it – we must, as believers, appropriate biblical principles into the circumstance, as well as allow the Holy Spirit to have control of our emotions and our mindset. God has made the availability of the Spirit, who is God, to take on the stress, so that we don't have to. I know, most of you are probably saying to yourself, "There is no way that I can experience stress-free living!" Well, if not totally stress-free, at least a minimized level of it if the flesh is able to stay out of the way.

Maybe people need to realize that there are three different types of stress. Is it possible that, because of many individuals' being emotional or over-thoughtful about circumstances, they create stress that is brought on by getting overly emotional, rather than by the situation itself? Unless you have had psychology at some point as a student or read it in a book or magazine or heard it on television, most people probably are not familiar with the three different types of stress. Let's take a quick look at them here:

- Acute stress – this stress is encountered daily with any work situation, conflict with people or things at home, or other areas in life. Acute stress, though carrying a negative connotation, actually brings about excitement.

Source (www.apa.org, nd)

An example of this type of stress I personally experienced recently while in Orlando, Florida. I was coaxed into getting on a swing that went over 100 feet in the air while the moving in a circular motion. What was a thrill initially, became a source of great stress. I couldn't wait until the ride ended; I will never get on a ride like that again! What made it a very stressful situation was having the wind blowing and the swing turning in all kinds of directions while going in the circle, including turning upside down where you could look down and see the ground below you. We were able to see how far up we were and it was quite scary; I was experiencing acute stress. Too much acute stress can bring about vomiting, tension, headaches, and other psychological and or physical symptoms. Emotionally, there might be anger, anxiety, irritability, and acute periods of depression.

- Episodic Stress – When acute stress occurs too frequently, it is called episodic stress. This stress is the type that many individuals are likely to have if it is occurring frequently. Episodic stress is usually seen in people who make self-inflicted, unrealistic or unreasonable demands that get tangled up and bring too much tension in their attempt to accomplish their personal or professional goals.

Source (www.apa.org, nd)

What is interesting about this type of stress is that it can typically be observed in those who are "Type A" personalities. People who are Type A's are overly competitive, aggressive, demanding and, sometimes, tense and hostile. Here are some of the symptoms of episodic stress that are found in Type A persons:

1. longer periods of intermittent depression, anxiety disorders and emotional distress
2. ceaseless worrying
3. persistent physical symptoms to those found in acute stress
4. coronary heart diseases, or other heart problems

Source (www.apa.org, nd)

- Chronic Stress – Chronic stress is opposite of acute stress. Where acute stress is exciting and thrilling, chronic stress is dangerous and unhealthy. Chronic stress will impact body, soul and spirit as well as mind. Chronic stress comes about through long-term exposure to stressors. These stressors are found in every part of life. Some of these situations involve unhappy marriages, traumatic experiences, an unwanted career or job, poverty, chronic illnesses, relationship conflicts, political differences, and dysfunctional families. Over time, continued stressful situations that just keep on accumulating can ultimately become life-threatening. Heart attacks, strokes, cancer, and psychological problems such as clinical depression and post-traumatic stress disorder (PTSD) can find their genesis from chronic stress. Some common physical signs and symptoms of chronic stress are: dry mouth, difficulty in breathing, pounding heart, stomach ache, headache, frequent urination, tightening of muscles, etc. Some mental signs and symptoms include sudden irritability, tension, problems with concentration, difficulty sleeping, narrowed perception, and frequent feelings of fatigue.

Source (www.apa.org, nd)

Understanding some of the different kinds of stress should help us to identify the stress type that we experience on a regular basis. Understanding what type of stress one has will determine what course of action should be taken.

I believe that one of the principles that we are able to extrapolate from this information about stress is that it indeed exists. The level of stress varies from person to person and job to job. What also comes into play is whether a person is able to apply biblical principles to their circumstances. Did you catch in the definition of episodic stress that a person brings a lot of it on themselves, that is, it's self-inflicted? Many people, especially in the workplace, have not built up an immunity spiritually that can protect them from the enemy's fiery darts that seem to be fixed on them on a regular basis. We haven't prepared our minds for battle as Peter says to do in I Peter Chapter 1. There seems to be an immaturity in the area of the emotions when it comes to many believers in general, let alone in the workplace. Notice how Jesus, throughout His earthly ministry, was under control emotionally. When He got angry, which is in the repertoire of emotions given by God, it was for a righteous purpose.

Remember the jobs that were listed earlier in this chapter that were the most stressful? They were stressful because they met the criteria that had been established by Career Cast. We were able to see that deadlines were at the top for most. Why is that? Is it because deadlines put people in a position of accountability? If so, should there really be a problem with it? Can a person change their mindset about deadlines and their response to them? The answer is yes. However, in the military when there is gunfire coming at a person, as well as roadside bombs that are hidden underground, a soldier must always be ready to move when the enemy attacks and be able to detect those bombs that have been planted. It is a life and death situation for these soldiers. Talk about stress! What about those individuals in Israel who never know when a bomb or rocket fire is going to come in their direction? Talk about living life on the edge! What about a police officer not knowing what to expect when he or she arrives on a call or when they pull over a car for a routine traffic stop? Talk about stress! A police officer or soldier must always maintain a mindset of readiness. If they don't, their lives could be over in a matter of seconds. Most of us will never know what it is like to encounter stressful situations like those in the military or on the police force. Most occupations do not know what it is like to experience that kind of pressure. So what we consider stressful situations for these other professions might be considered laughable. The issue then, I would think, is the mindset of those who are looking at their situations and creating the stress that appears to be attached to the job, but really it isn't. You've heard the saying that "perception is reality." Well, stress for some could actually be the *perceived reality* of stress. Their emotions could be tricking them into thinking that the job situation is stressful when in actuality the job itself isn't.

When we look at Scripture and consider some highly stressful situations, one must wonder, "What if God wasn't with those who He called to accomplish His will. How could they hold up on their own?" Just thinking from this perspective should cause you to consider looking at your situations and circumstances differently. Let's look at some of these biblical circumstances.

Can you imagine Moses going before Pharaoh and asking him to let the people go without God's presence giving him what he needed to stand before a man of such stature? What about Joshua when he entered into the promise land? God came to him and told him to have courage, courage that would be needed to face giants in the land. What about Elijah when he called down fire on the false prophets? What about Gideon when God found him in a wine press hiding? God spoke truth into him and he walked out of that wine press to lead the nation of Israel as a judge. In the New Testament, we see what happens when Jesus leaves the earth and the Holy Spirit arrives. His disciples receive power that enables them to do things that only God can do through them. That same power has been given to us today. But are we walking and living in it? Peter was bold in speaking truth to the Jews. Why? Because the presence of God gave him what he needed to accomplish the will of God. How about Paul? His life was in jeopardy his entire ministry. What stress Paul would have and should have felt! He was literally running for his life several times, and even was at the point of death a few times. Look at the description that Paul gives us in 2 Corinthians Chapter 11:

2 Corinthians 11:16-33 (AMP)

16 I repeat then, let no one think I have lost my wits; but even if you do, then bear with a witless man, so that I too may boast a little.
17 What I say by way of this confident boasting, I say not with the Lord's authority [by inspiration] but, as it were, in pure witlessness.
18 [For] since many boast of worldly things *and* according to the flesh, I will glory (boast) also. 19 For you readily *and* gladly bear with the foolish, since you are so smart *and* wise yourselves!
20 For you endure it if a man assumes control of your souls *and* makes slaves of you, or devours [your substance, spends your money] *and* preys upon you, or deceives *and* takes advantage of you, or is arrogant *and* puts on airs, or strikes you in the face.

21 To my discredit, I must say, we have shown ourselves too weak [for you to show such tolerance of us and for us to do strong, courageous things like that to you]! But in whatever any person is bold *and* dares [to boast]—mind you, I am speaking in this foolish (witless) way—I also am bold *and* dare [to boast].

22 They are Hebrews? So am I! They are Israelites? So am I! They are descendants of Abraham? So am I!

23 Are they [ministering] servants of Christ (the Messiah)? I am talking like one beside himself, [but] I am more, with far more extensive *and* abundant labors, with far more imprisonments, [beaten] with countless stripes, and frequently [at the point of] death.

24 Five times I received from [the hands of] the Jews forty [lashes all] but one;

25 Three times I have been beaten with rods; once I was stoned. Three times I have been aboard a ship wrecked at sea; a [whole] night and a day I have spent [adrift] on the deep;

26 Many times on journeys, [exposed to] perils from rivers, perils from bandits, perils from [my own] nation, perils from the Gentiles, perils in the city, perils in the desert places, perils in the sea, perils from those posing as believers [but destitute of Christian knowledge and piety];

27 In toil and hardship, watching often [through

sleepless nights], in hunger and thirst, frequently driven to fasting by want, in cold and exposure *and* lack of clothing.

28 And besides those things that are without, there is the daily [inescapable pressure] of my care *and* anxiety for all the churches!

29 Who is weak, and I do not feel [his] weakness? Who is made to stumble *and* fall *and* have his faith hurt, and I am not on fire [with sorrow or indignation]?

30 If I must boast, I will boast of the things that [show] my infirmity [of the things by which I am made weak and contemptible in the eyes of my opponents].

31 The God and Father of the Lord Jesus *Christ* knows, He Who is blessed *and* to be praised forevermore, that I do not lie.

32 In Damascus, the city governor acting under King Aretas guarded the city of Damascus [on purpose] to arrest me,

33 And I was [actually] let down in a [rope] basket *or* hamper through a window (a small door) in the wall, and I escaped through his fingers.

Can you even imagine the stressful life that Paul must have had while doing the job that God called him to do, which was to be a missionary and an itinerant preacher? Most lives that we live do not even come close to what he dealt with on a daily basis fulfilling the will and the plan of God.

How about the Ultimate Person, Jesus Himself who displays, I believe, His greatest emotional trial when in the garden of Gethsemane? There, Jesus displayed true humanity when agonizing about going to the cross. Can you imagine the weight of that stress? The entire weight of sin from every person who ever existed and who ever would exist would be upon His shoulders. But in the moment, Jesus realized it was about the will of God; He was to fulfill His purpose. That moment sheds light on how to face stress at a deeper level in our lives. Is what we do at work about fulfilling the will of God?

Jesus was fulfilling his job assignment; He was working. His work, though stressful, would probably fit into the category of being the most stressful job ever in the history of humankind. Jesus dispelled the stress of Passion Week by His obedience to the Father. Yes, we can deal with stress using the various methods that are suggested by psychologists and counselors. Stress can be managed through meditation, yoga, squeezing a ball, beating a boxing bag or pillow, going for a run or jog, or listening to music. All these things can help us manage stress. But what about coming to a place in our lives where we can live and be stress free; how do we do that? We do it by allowing the Holy Spirit to have total control of our lives and surrendering our emotions to Him. The other thing is to be walking in the will of God on a regular basis. He tells us that in Him we find rest. Let's trade our stress for His rest in every matter in life.

Chapter 11

THE IMPORTANCE OF SELF-CARE

AMERICA IS ONE OF THE BUSIEST COUNTRIES IN THE ENTIRE WORLD. THERE are other countries that would fit into the same category as the USA when it comes to business, however. When we talk about business, we are talking about a life that is focused on work. There is a great deal of time associated with the work that individuals are performing. There are many individuals who work two or more jobs as well, some even more. Between all the jobs together, a person might work over 12 hours per day. The purpose of all this time devoted to the workplace, of course, varies from family to family. Some work extra hours to be able to help make ends meet. Some work extra hours just because they can. If a person is single with not much responsibility, it is possible for that person to have a desire to work as much as possible just because they want to. Some work additional hours because they want to purchase something that is expensive or that is much desired, and they need to save in order to get whatever that item might be. Still others work because they are in debt. In addition, there are those who work because they love saving money. We also need to realize that there are many entrepreneurs who put in long hours in order to grow the business they started. They believe it is necessary to put in long hours every day if the business is going to succeed. In most cases, those business owners are correct; sacrifice is essential if the business is going to make it. It is necessary to realize that there is a cost for that decision of investing in a business, however. Most business plans require the investment of the profits generated be placed back into the business at least for the first 3 to 5 years. The startup costs for many businesses range from between $500,000 to $2,000,000. That means what would be considered profit is not truly profit; it is money that is reinvested into the businesses in order for it to grow and eventually become a profit-producing enterprise.

I was having a conversation recently with someone at the Masonic Village, a senior living facility where I serve as chaplain. We were discussing the subject of work. I mentioned to her that when I worked for the City of Philadelphia, I would take 3 vacations per year. The person, who happened to be female, immediately stated that she never went on vacations. She represents those from a certain era of time who really didn't believe in taking vacations. It is unfortunate that many chose to work most of their lives and never wanted to vacation until after retirement. Many who had plans for retirement to travel weren't able to do so because of health problems or other reasons that materialized during their retirement. However, we now know that vacations are necessary and should be used. There are some jobs that should include mental health days because of the type of work that is being performed. Some employers might provide them, but most do not.

I remember when I first started working over 35 years ago that my mindset was like the woman I was speaking to that day. I wasn't even considering taking a vacation at the time I was first employed. I thought it was a badge of honor to *not* take off. However, as time went on, my mindset began to change in regards to vacations and taking time off. Going on vacation is part of self-care. The Scripture lets us know that God created the Sabbath and one of the purposes of sabbath is for rest. Yes, we know that it is set aside for the worship of God on that day, but it is also for the purpose of a day where one can rest from regular work that would be taking place. For individuals who work on the day that most worship, especially those who lead the people in worship, the sabbath must be another day of the week. A vacation provides a sabbath from work. Being able to get away from the job and to totally focus on something other than work is quite helpful for one's mind. Even in sports, most players come out of the game to get a rest or, if it is baseball, the manager will give a superstar a night off at some point.

Rest is necessary for recuperation of the mind and body. There is quite a bit of energy needed for the mind to continuously be active. When the mind is constantly in the mode of thinking, at some point it gets tired. The mind needs rest, just like the body when pushed on a regular basis. I decided several years ago that when my vacation time went from 4 weeks to 5 weeks per year, I would take 3 vacations per year to actually go away somewhere. When I use the term "go away," I am talking about going to another city, town, or country, literally changing locations. A change of scenery does wonders for the mind. There is something that is uplifting when there is a different scene for our minds to take in. Since our kids were being homeschooled and my wife, Bev, was home most of the day, we were able to go on vacation 3 times per year. We would go on a trip with the kids twice, usually in the

Spring and Fall, and then Bev and I would go on a vacation without the kids in the fall. We would have quality time together without the kids, spending that time enjoying each other and strengthening our relationship as a couple. Many couples don't consider getting away, especially without children, to be important for the marriage, but it truly is. It is so easy to get caught up in the routine of business week after week and, when that happens, relationships with each other can get lost. Taking a break from work and the business will help realign the relationships. How? When one is able to rest body soul, spirit and mind, one can actually gauge where things are in the family in regards to importance at that point in time. Having a pause in work will allow us to see things in our lives that might not be seen due to the business. Not only was the time off helpful mentally every 4 months for us, it was beneficial for Bev because of her daily teaching of the children. Having that break from the daily grind of school provided an opportunity for her to regenerate mentally and emotionally. Just think: if most people would begin to incorporate this principle of vacation into their lives every year, it could help not only their psyche, but their relationships as well.

To be honest, it was the purchase of a time share that got us to begin going away on vacation consistently. And, just to be clear, stay-cations aren't the same. A person will usually find stuff to do around the house should they take time off from work and stay home or near home. This is just a different type of work. A vacation *away* from home will produce the greater possibility of getting rest, both mentally and emotionally. Incorporating activities such as going to the beach, going hiking, visiting famous places, or just sitting down reading a book or listening to music helps the mind and body to relax. A good word to use is "escape" – that is, to escape the daily pressures and issues of work. We should never take our work with us on vacation; it is *vacation*! Someone else can take on your responsibility for the week.

Is there a definition for self-care? I guess we can use the words that are in the word itself. It is the care of oneself. It sounds so basic, and yet it can be difficult for many people. As Americans, the tendency is to overdo things. We have the propensity to want a lot of things in life, specifically material possessions. Our country thrives on debt and, since things are so easy to buy with credit, we don't have to wait to get it. In fact, debt is encouraged over savings. The country really doesn't encourage savings. There are individuals, when it comes to credit cards, who find themselves in major consumer debt. When it comes to managing credit cards, many individuals are very poor at doing so. We are able to see that people become enslaved to the debt, and then they have to work to pay off that debt, which can take several years. As the Bible says, the person in debt becomes a slave to the lender. A mindset to work all the time without considering taking breaks leads to increased tension, irritability and tiredness over time. As the string of work days continues, burnout can now begin to raise its head in a person's life. Burnout doesn't have to occur when the proper balance of work and rest is in place.

Self-care also includes proper diet, exercise, and management of stress. Let me say something up front: Self-care is not being selfish; self-care is recognizing the need for you to give yourself what is needed so that you can be at maximum potential for producing what is needed for your job or for other people. Self-care helps everyone that is dependent upon you. For example, when you look at a stay-at-home mom and wife – which we call today a "domestic engineer" – we know that most wives and moms tend to be sacrificial in nature. These women, as well as those who work and come home to do things after work, just keep going and going. However, it is necessary for a woman to have "me-time" – that is, time allowed for her to get away from her normal routine. Things like going shopping (for herself and *not* groceries), getting her hair done, getting her nails done, going out with the girls, or going to visit a friend. Whatever they decide to do, they need sabbath at some point a few days a week in their schedule. One of the things that Bev used to do often to get "me-time" during the week was to go the CVS or Rite Aid for about an hour to walk the aisles. She used this time to get out of the house for a change of scenery. When self-care isn't a part of a person's regular routine, there will be more emotional manifestations in their life that will be negative. Another word that is used is balance. We will usually associate balance with people who work too much. The proclivity is to minimize the need for rest; it is put on the back burner and considered not to be something productive.

I was watching the movie, The Ten Commandments, the eve before Easter Sunday. There was a scene in the movie where Pharaoh is having the Israelites work 7 days a week. In addition, they were not being given the proper amount of food. Because of this kind of treatment, they were weak and many were dying. Moses, who was in power as a prince over the building projects, made the decision to give them a day off every week and to allow them access to the grain in the storage bins that were being saved for idols who couldn't eat it anyway. What we see in this example is that when Moses gave them a day of rest and food, the Israelites were able to be more productive. This is a scene that was in a movie, but it makes the point that I want to convey, that it is true in our lives. Rest and nourishment will result in an increase in productivity on our jobs.

I heard on the radio this morning that one of the local school districts is changing the time for classes to start for their middle school students. The research that apparently was conducted showed that if children have a later start time for school, they will be better able to focus on their school work. It will also help them to stay awake in the classroom. The later starting time will also help them get extra rest that they currently are not able to get. I hope that they are correct with this assessment. To me, if parents would put their kids to bed early enough so that the children could get the amount of sleep needed, that would make the difference in alertness of the children in the mornings. In addition, is it possible that the school is giving too much homework to the kids, which also has an impact on the bedtime schedule? Just a couple additional thoughts here: The students might just stay up even later if they don't have to be to school until a later time. And, to me, this is really an issue of self-care. For children, self-care must be taught by their parents. I believe that the onus falls on the parents as opposed to the schools with regard to the children's sleep schedule.

Self-care, when it comes to sleep is also important for employees. I realize that some people don't need a lot of sleep, but it is important that the body gets the chance to rest. Some people have to get a certain amount of sleep each night or they are no good the next day. Some jobs require alertness and focus. If that is not present, the possibility/potential for someone getting hurt is increased. Sleep allows the body to regenerate in many areas while providing healing in other areas. Lack of sleep can also cause individuals to be short tempered and irritable. Feeling refreshed in the morning will set the tone for the day and also prepare the person to handle situations that may easily be impacted emotionally if they are lacking sleep. When we get the proper amount of sleep each night, production in the workplace will be up. There are some individuals who suffer with insomnia; they are functional, but there will be times that production might be impacted due to their lack of sleep. Of course, depending on what type of work is being performed, sleep will have an effect in varying degrees

Another area of self-care is mental health. It is crucial that people are able to function in what is considered to be a normal manner. When there are obvious emotional changes that occur out of nowhere and begin to occur frequently, something adverse mentally might be going on. It is crucial to let someone who is a supervisor know so that the appropriate steps can be taken. Mental health issues can wreak havoc in the workplace if left unchecked. Nipping an issue in the bud by getting the person help is crucial in neutralizing the negative impact in a workplace environment. I recall having co-workers who were suffering from depression, some suffering from PTSD and some who were suffering from bipolar disorder. In fact, anxiety disorder was another condition that I believed was present. What are the common disorders that affect mood, thinking and behavior?

- Clinical Depression – is a mental health disorder characterized by persistently depressed mood or lack of interest in activities, causing significant impairment in daily life

- Anxiety Disorder – a mental disorder characterized by feelings of worry, anxiety or fear that are strong enough to interfere with one's daily activities.
- Bipolar Disorder – a disorder associated with episodes of radical mood swings ranging from depressive lows to manic highs
- PTSD – A disorder in which a person has difficulty recovering after experiencing or witnessing a traumatic event.

Source (www.adaa.org, nd)

The above disorders affect over 12 million people a year, with each disorder impacting approximately 3 million each (www.google.com, most common types of mental disorders, nd). One in four people in the world will be affected by mental or neurological disorders at some point in their lives. Around 450 million people currently suffer from such conditions, placing mental disorders among the leading causes of ill health and disability worldwide. Treatments are available, but ony two thirds of people with a known mental disorders ever seek help from a health professional. Stigma, discrimination and neglect prevent care and treatment from reaching people with mental disorders, says the worldwide Health Organization (WHO).

Source (www.who.int)

If one in four individuals have a mental disorder at some point in their lives, there will always be someone in the workplace that will have mental issues occurring. Individuals with any one of these disorders are in various types of jobs across the country. Some most likely are at your place of employment. It is quite predictable that there will be some individuals at our places of employment who will display the symptoms from one of the above disorders. All of the disorders, except for bipolar disorder, are curable when treated. Bipolar disorder can be managed with medication, but not cured. If a believer displays any of these disorders, they should have a desire to be as whole as possible. What I mean by "whole" is that a believer should want to do whatever is necessary and possible to be able to function at 100%. There are many individuals who will live in denial, including people of faith, and refuse to get the help needed because they feel that they are okay. Denial, or the refusal to get help when people are constantly telling the person that their behavior is inappropriate is, in essence, refusing help and staying in a position emotionally that is unhealthy. Self-care in this situation is getting the necessary help so that the person is able to function at what is considered to be a normal manner.

Another aspect of self-care is knowing how to control emotions. This is a learned behavior and we talked about this quite a bit in an earlier chapter. Not allowing people to get under your skin is so important. If learned, this ability alone can keep our hearts and minds safe, as well as help us in experiencing very little stress. Part of keeping the emotions in check is not to keep thinking about the stuff that happens to us. When our thinking continues to focus on the things that occurred in our lives that were negative, we are misusing our energy and not helping our minds to change the results that came from the circumstances encountered. Keeping short accounts of the issues in our lives and the things that people do to us will help us to keep our minds clear and focused on the things that are worthwhile. Remember what Philippians 4:8-9 says.

8 Finally, brothers, whatever is true, whatever is noble, whatever is right, whatever is pure, whatever is lovely, whatever is admirable--if anything is excellent or praiseworthy--think about such things.

9 Whatever you have learned or received or heard from me, or seen in me--put it into practice. And the God of peace will be with you.

Another self-care issue that I believe is important has to do with drinking alcohol. I understand that people drink socially; however, what most consider social is really on the borderline of being an alcoholic. Most will be in denial regarding this area. When you drink every day, what most people consider to be occasional then becomes a regular routine. Whether a person wants to believe it or not, over time, drinking alcohol regularly will impact the mind and, thereby, that person's judgment. The Scripture lets us know that we are to be sober in our judgment; in other words, we should exhibit sound judgment. Can we say that people who drink regularly are making good, sound decisions in their lives? This is a part of self-care that many individuals do not consider. Having a buzz will have an impact on the mind and will hinder a person's judgment.

The final thought in regards to self-care is to have individuals in your life to talk with about issues of concern. Being able to converse with others who can be objective is a necessity in our lives. When we try to handle things on our own, especially when we have been impacted emotionally, we need to have another voice speak that is outside of our head. We tend to believe what we think and, when connected with emotion, we can arrive at the wrong conclusion. Wise people in our circle can help monitor our thinking and can help us stay grounded emotionally. People who play this type of role are of great value, and appreciating these type of people will let them know the importance of the role they play in our lives. Of course, the individuals need to know the Lord if we are talking about receiving the wisdom of God. Being with wise people will help us to become wiser.

The Scriptures talk about loving one self. This love isn't one that is egotistical or selfish but one that is a proper self-assessment of ourselves. That is what it means to examine ourselves; we look at our lives and assess what is needed. We ask others to give their opinion as well concerning what they see in our lives. When filtered through God's Spirit, we are able to determine what areas need work. This is the spiritual aspect of self-care. Jesus exercised self-care as He balanced His life with the work of ministry, the time He spent with His disciples, the time He spent with His friends, and the time He spent with His Father. As we observe the life of Jesus, He shows us the example of how to approach life and to establish balance. The discipline of self-care is essential for us if we want to maximize our potential for the kingdom as well as our work.

Chapter 12

STANDING ALONE

I HAVE A FRIEND WHO HAS ALWAYS BEEN SINGLE. SHE HAS PLENTY OF friends and has had them for several years. She has been able to do everything that she has wanted to do in life. For many people, singleness is extremely difficult. Let's be real: Most individuals who might remain single, even though they are believers, do not live lives of abstinence. I am sure she has had her moments, but she has been content with her singleness. The point I want to make here is that she is alone, but not lonely. Although she lives in a house by herself – and by the way, she owns it – she has handled all of her affairs throughout her life responsibly. She has never been moved to do what other people do or what the crowd might have wanted her to do. She has stood strong over the years, and has exercised an extreme amount of discipline and integrity. She is living a life that is pleasing to God and one that is fulfilling to her. No one is helping her to live a life like this. She is standing alone. No one can live her life for her; she is not impacted by those individuals who might ask her, "Why aren't you married yet?"

It seems that when it comes to integrity in our day, that the culture considers it not to be that important. The culture surely does not promote it. To be honest, it is hard to find integrity as a whole in most places, including houses of faith. It is really not being emphasized that much anymore. Integrity is a term that can describe a person who I would consider to be very dependable with their life. A person with integrity is able to be trusted and, for the most part, will make thoughtful and responsible decisions. But what is integrity really? Integrity is the quality of being honest and having strong moral principles, moral uprightness.

I bring this word integrity out to the forefront because, as a believer, this quality should characterize one's life. The Scriptures even say that this quality is important in a person's life. Let's look at some of those Scriptures that makes it quite clear.

- **Proverbs 11:3** The integrity of the upright guides them, but the unfaithful are destroyed by their duplicity.
- **2 Corinthians 8:21** For we are taking pains to do what is right, not only in the eyes of the Lord but also in the eyes of men.
- **Hebrews 13:18** Pray for us. We are sure that we have a clear conscience and desire to live honorably in every way.
- **Psalm 41:11-12** I know that you are pleased with me, for my enemy does not triumph over me. 12 In my integrity you uphold me and set me in your presence forever.
- **Proverbs 21:3** To do what is right and just is more acceptable to the LORD than sacrifice.

What is the common denominator with these verses? They all point to doing what is right. Integrity encompasses a mindset of always wanting to do the right thing. Doing the right thing with the right motive in the power of God brings glory to Him. I thought it was appropriate to open this chapter using my friend's lifestyle as a genuine Christian single to present to you an example of standing alone. It is a picture of standing alone for the purpose of pleasing God. However, she is standing with God being alongside of her, through the Spirit. That is one of the ministries of the Holy Spirit; He is the "one who walks along side." She serves as a great example of what it is to live a life of singleness with integrity. She has been upright and moral, despite temptations. She has been able to stand alone even when *being* alone. She was able to exhibit integrity in the midst of being by herself, a position where she could have opened the door to the enemy in her life to have a field day. We are able to see that she exhibits character. I once heard the definition for character as "what a person is by themselves when nobody is around." In other words, the values and behaviors that are visible when the person is in public doesn't change when they are alone. This quality of being able to exhibit character no matter when or where or who is around is due to integrity. That means that my friend is the same whether in a place of employment, at home, at church, or anywhere in the public.

Integrity is what makes a person able to stand by themselves; it is this quality that helps them not to do what the other employees may be doing. It is this quality that helps a person to be honest about things, especially when the pressure is on not to be truthful or honest. It is the quality of integrity that considers the other person before oneself. But this quality of integrity isn't valued in the workplace these days, although it was a quality that was highly acknowledged for many years. However, in our current culture, the degree to which it is an important quality of an employee is no longer primary. There seems to be an acceptance of individuals having a degree of dishonesty as opposed to honesty, and many will sell their souls on behalf of lies that are told. There are work environments that thrive on dishonesty and it is expected that the employees buy into this type of culture. For a believer, if we find ourselves in that kind of environment, we should want to get out of it, and to get out of it as soon as possible. By staying in an environment that is purposely initiating dishonest practices, we will be compromising our faith and will put ourselves in a situation that could bring about consequences with the law. Being a person of integrity in the workplace might not earn us recognition from people or get us an award, but it will be pleasing to God, who is ultimately the One who we are desiring, or should be, desiring to please.

There were several situations in which I took the heat for my employees of which they weren't even aware. For example, there were times that an employee technically should have been disciplined for something that they failed or had forgotten to do. I was told to write them up (give them discipline on paper.) I was to discipline them for what they didn't do, but because I was made aware of the circumstances, I would fight for them behind the scenes so that they wouldn't get the write up. I would even take the blame for it at times because I wasn't on top of them to get it done. They had no idea that I had taken the weight for what they had done by not giving them a write up. Why would I choose to exercise this type of action? What would be a justifiable reason for me to do such a thing? It was because I knew my co-workers well enough to know that there had to be a good explanation as to why they failed to do it. These employees that I would usually do this for were reliable, dependable, and trustworthy. I didn't mind standing for them because of those qualities that they had displayed consistently. These consistent qualities were indicators that they were employees who I could count on and if they had a bad day, which was few and far between, I was going to grant them grace. If I felt that discipline wasn't deserved or warranted, I would state my reasons to my director.

There were also times that I was told to write someone up and intentionally didn't do it. In most cases, my superior forgot about it. As a manager, I felt it was necessary to evaluate the situations properly and not be moved by the emotion of someone else or by my emotions when considering discipline. It is important that when we look at this example of standing alone, we have to understand what the genuine motive is for us to take an action or not in regards to discipline. It was not because I wanted favor from my guys or wanted them to like me; rather it was for the purpose of being what I considered to be right with my co-workers. My decisions were being determined by my faith in God and how I viewed the situations through the grid of Scripture that was operating in my life. I truly was looking at each situation by itself and not just taking an action because I was told to do so. I hope that you can see this is a major thought process of attempting to be a servant leader in the workplace as a person who is in a position of authority. As you were able to see in a previous chapter, I administered disciplinary action when it was totally necessary.

With the type of work that I was involved with on a regular basis with the city, there would always be opportunities for overtime. When overtime was necessary in the workplace, there was a time when we, as managers, would be able to choose who we wanted for the overtime situations. (When Fairmount Park and The Department of Recreation merged, the policy for overtime changed.)

Overtime for many employees became a lifestyle. There were employees who were very dependable; they not only were available to work overtime on short notice, but they actually *worked* during the overtime hours. There were employees who would want to work overtime but didn't necessarily work when given the opportunity arose. Why would I want employees to come in for overtime if they weren't going to do the work that was needed? Choosing employees wasn't about favoritism, although there were some managers who appeared to be operating that way; it was about dependability. For me, I would make every effort to act justly in regards to how the overtime was distributed. Many people use the term "fair" in the workplace. They will quickly try to ascertain whether a person is being fair or not. I never liked that term "fair" because the term is relative. People have different meanings or perspectives as to what they believe "fair" to mean. If an employee wasn't being productive during regular work hours, why would I want to bring them into work for overtime purposes? Talk about standing alone! Employees always complained about who was working overtime. There were many occasions where I was accused of not distributing overtime fairly. Again, it wasn't a question of fairness; it was a question of dependability as well as the capability and capacity of the person to perform particular functions. Depending on the overtime job, I would need specific employees to perform in specific areas; all employees weren't needed. Employees still complained, despite my telling them how the needs for the overtime were being assessed. For example, if we were going to work on baseball fields, I would need a person who would be able to drive the truck that was hauling infield mix, a person who could operate the tractor, and two or three grounds guys. That is a total of 5 men for a ball field. The number of employees would be limited depending on how much was left in the budget for that time of year, which happened to be spring. The employees who were equipment operators would be in more demand than the grounds workers. Why? Because of their ability to operate the equipment. The more skills a person had, the more valuable of an employee they would be. Unfortunately, some employees just would not understand that. So for me, again, despite being accused of being unfair and discriminatory with who I brought in for overtime, it was a question of being just, which was emanating from integrity. It was not because I was helping an employee build up his or her pension or because I liked one person over another. What I was doing and how I was doing it was evolving out of my relationship with Jesus and the use of the principles of God's Word to guide my decision making.

Standing alone in the workplace, I must admit, can be lonely. There are feelings of isolation, feelings of abandonment and sometimes, by upper management, and feelings of being misunderstood. There are also feelings of anger due to how people perceive you, and feelings of hatred that can be toward those who are making false accusations about you to others. There are individuals who are co-workers who will intentionally spread lies about you. For a believer, this type of behavior by co-workers is to be expected

139

when living out your faith on the job. Don't get me wrong, I am not saying that I wanted it to happen; I am saying that is to be expected. Why? Most employees' mindsets are not going to be governed by Christian principles. The majority of employees whom believers will be around most of the time will be those who might have some moral compass, but will generally be operating out of what the Bible would term as "the flesh." People are taught to look out for themselves at an early age. Most are not taught how to be concerned for the other person. The values that come from the pages of Holy Writ are foolishness to most individuals, because only the God in us can help us to implement those principles, as well as understand them.

Being able to stand in the midst of the enemy that is all around you actually should be the norm. Let us be reminded of the wisdom that comes from the 23rd Psalm, a Psalm of David. David is known as the shepherd king. He knew what it was like to stand alone, being the youngest at the time who was watching the sheep. He was all alone, literally by himself with the sheep, while his brothers were doing other things. God, however, was preparing him to be a king, even though at the time he was a shepherd watching sheep. He would not only shepherd sheep but, eventually, he would shepherd people as the king. David, who went though many hardships in his life, including being on the run from King Saul who was jealous of him, ultimately fulfilled the plan of God by being the king of Israel and establishing the throne of David.

David penned the words, "Thou preparest a table before me in the presence of mine enemies." in Psalm 23. Just take those words and allow them to permeate your mind for a minute. Picture your enemies being all around you desiring you dead, and you are sitting down in their midst at a table eating a meal that your best friend has prepared for you. That doesn't make any sense. We must remember that David literally found himself in this position. That is why he is able to write these words; he actually experienced it. We also see David as a boy confront the enemy of Israel in the person of Goliath. Most have heard the story of David and Goliath. David was the only one who was willing to stand against Goliath, who was a mighty Philistine warrior. No soldier from the Israelite army wanted to face him; in fact, the army as a whole didn't not want to face this warrior. Goliath was the Philistines' greatest hero and no one had been able to stand against him. That was the case, until little David came along with a great faith in a powerful God. David, knowing that he was in the will of God – walking in the power of God, trusting in the ability of God – went out and faced the giant with a rock and a slingshot. He knew that the presence of God was with him; that Friend who was standing with him was God. I am able to be in the midst of my enemies when I know that God is with me. As a believer, I know He is with me because he lives in me. John says in I John 4:4 " You, dear children, are from God and have overcome them, because the one who is in you is greater than the one who is in the world." That is how we are able to stand alone at work. We know that His presence is with us, especially when we know we are walking in truth.

In an earlier chapter, I talked about being able to stand alone, especially when being pressured by co-workers to go to office parties or out for drinks after work. If one doesn't feel comfortable, you need to be honest and not do it; no one is holding a gun to your head. In such situations, integrity will help a person be able not to submit to peer pressure but to God's will in that moment. Peer pressure, whether experienced as a teenager in high school or as an adult in the workplace, is the same. When we yield to the pressure, basically we are doing something mainly because others want us to do it. We are satisfying the desire that is within us to please them or to be accepted by them. When this type of behavior is manifesting in our lives, the behavior is feeding into a deeper issue within us. Being accepted by our peers or trying to please people has to do with how we feel about ourselves. This is a self-image problem. We need to be honest with ourselves, if this is indeed why we are making decisions based upon what others want. The tendency is for most individuals to give in to their peers. We don't want to feel left out or thought of as a party pooper. However, if I do not make a decision that is made completely of my own choosing, then I am being controlled by the feelings of my peers. Peer pressure is control. As a believer in Jesus, I need to be led by God's Spirit and not by the pressure placed on me by others. This applies to every area of life, not just the workplace.

There was a time in church that I had to stand when it came to something I believed God wanted me to do. I had gone to the pastor about it and a week later, he wanted to see me about it. He told me that God did not speak to him about what I knew God was speaking to *me* about. I had to tell him that it is not out of disrespect that I say this but, "I know what God is telling me to do." I proceeded to plan what it was. It was time to leave that church and begin to do ministry in the neighborhood where I lived, which was the Roxborough section of Philadelphia. There was another time when God had put on my heart to start a ministry of counseling. There were a few people who approached us (Bev and I) who asked if we have permission from the pastor. We kindly told them that we didn't need to get permission from the pastor to do what God wanted. However, we did inform the pastor of our intentions. In the church setting, there are many times that the pastor of a church will feel that what you do in your life regarding spiritual issues must come through them. Accountability to leadership in the church is important and is biblical. However, the decision by a person should not be based solely on how the pastor feels or thinks. There is wisdom with a multitude of counselors, according to Solomon in Proverbs. Also, there will be times where God will have you do something that everyone else in your circle does not agree with, yet God wants you to do it. In such a case, you must stand alone in order to be obedient to God.

Standing alone can be difficult even when you are in obedience to God because everybody isn't going to get it. People are at different places in their relationship with God, with some not even knowing what it is to hear His voice. There will be times in life where you will be standing alone in regards to an issue with a spouse. The pastor could be standing alone in regards to the direction of the church with the leadership body. An executive director of a company might be at odds with the members of the board on an issue. A student might have to stand alone in a class room setting where everyone accepts what the professor says except them. Standing alone is a consistent posture across the board with a person because of the integrity that is present in their life. When a person stands alone, they are standing for what they know to be truth for them. They are convicted and are willing to endure the backlash, cruelty, negative actions and attitudes of those who do not accept their freedom of choice.

Standing alone is not always an easy thing to do; for most, it is extremely difficult. The purpose isn't to have people be upset with you or to go against them personally. The real purpose is doing the right thing for you. If that right thing is to please God, then taking a stand is the way to please Him. Jesus walked the earth surrounded by people who initially loved Him, those who hated Him, those who didn't like the things he said, those who were jealous of Him and those who truly loved Him. He did not concern Himself with what Paul refers to as "civilian matters." He was focused on the path to the cross. If He had listened to others, He would have never made it to the cross, and might have changed the direction that His Father had given Him. But because of Who He was, He was able to stand alone. In fact, Jesus *was* alone. Only He could have made it all the way to the finish line of the cross. We are able to stand, because He was able to stand. How? Through the power of the Spirit. When you have done all that you can, what do you do? Stand!

Chapter 13

AMATEUR OR PROFESSIONAL

IF YOU ARE ANYTHING LIKE ME, WHEN IT COMES TO YOUR HOUSE BEING nice and comfortable, warm and cozy, and a place that you look forward to coming home to every day, you will do whatever is necessary to create that environment. Some people, when purchasing a new house – at least being new to them – will have the house remodeled to their liking. There have been thousands and thousands of couples who have intentionally purchased a house and then had it remodeled. Why? In many cases, they liked the layout of the of house but might not have liked certain parts of it, like the kitchen or bathroom or the aesthetics. Affordability was not an issue. That is how we got our first house. After delaying our purchase for approximately two years, we found out from a friend that his father was putting his aunt's house up for sale, as she had recently passed away. She had a house on a small street in Roxborough that was being sold for $30,000. Because he knew about it and also knew we were in search of a property, he made it known to us. It was a fixer upper, but it was a house in an area where we wanted to be.

When Bev first saw the house, she was thoroughly disgusted. Aesthetically speaking, it was horrendous; every room had issues. The wallpaper was yellow and ripped with several areas being held together by tape. The dining room had a window in the middle of the wall that separated the dining room from the kitchen. The kitchen had no cabinets with an old-fashioned washing machine with the rollers at the top was sitting in the middle of the floor. Upstairs were two bedrooms with the second room being an open space with no storage. You had to walk through the open bedroom to get to the bathroom, which had a claw-legged bathtub that was 5 ft. long. After going through several conversations with Bev, we came to a decision to purchase the property. I kept telling her that she needed to have vision and that we would renovate the house to our liking. My friend, who was quite handy, offered to start work on it. This house was old and small. The original size of the house was even smaller than what it was currently. Two rooms, one being a kitchen and the other a shed kitchen, were add-ons. That is why the window was in the wall between the dining room and the kitchen.

When people get their houses renovated, they have several options from which to choose, first being that the homeowner could have the skills to do it themselves. Second, the owner could have another person who has the skills do it, even though they might not have a business license or is not part of a construction company. They are known as handy men; we would be called amateurs. The third option is to have a professional do it. This would be a person who has a business and is licensed and bonded and would have examples of their work to show to their customers. For the majority of individuals, income level, as well as the budget most likely would determine who they hire to perform the remodeling work.

Did you notice the two types of people – other than the home-owner – that I mentioned above? The first was an amateur and the second was a professional. We hear these terms quite often when it comes to sports. We associate amateur sports with college or any level played where the athletes do not get remuneration for what they do. Even athletes in the Olympics, at least several years ago, were considered amateur athletes which meant they could not have been getting paid in order to participate in the games. Things changed with the Olympics several years ago in the Olympic sport of basketball and hockey, however. The 1992 USA basketball team was called the "Dream Team," and that team was comprised of basketball players from the NBA which, of course, is a professional basketball league. The sport of hockey began using professional hockey players for their Olympic teams as opposed to those at the college level. As to the other sports, athletes who were being sponsored by companies were still considered amateur athletes.

The question that should be asked is, "What is the real difference between an amateur and a professional?" Is it really just the money that makes a difference or does the money really matter? We are able to see that there are a few meanings for each in the dictionary. They are:

Amateur – 1. a person who engages in a pursuit, especially a sport, on an unpaid rather than a professional basis. Synonym – layman, non-professional

2. a person who is incompetent or inept at a particular activity – unskilled, inept one who engages in a pursuit, study, science, or sport as a pastime rather than a profession.

Source (www.google.com)

147

Professional 1. relating to or connected with a profession

2. engaged in a specified activity as one's main paid occupation rather than a pastime.

Source (www.google.com)

Professional Employee – engaged in work, predominantly intellectual and varied in character as opposed to routine mental, manual, mechanical, or physical work, involving the consistent exercise of discretion and judgment in its performance; of such a character that the output produced or the result accomplished cannot be standardized in relation to a given period of time; requiring knowledge of an advanced type in a field of science or learning customarily acquired by a prolonged course of specialized intellectual instruction and study in an institution of higher learning or a hospital, as distinguished from a general academic education, or from a general academic education or from an apprenticeship or from training in the performance of routine mental, manual, or physical processes.

Source (https://www.lectlaw.com/def2/p095.htm)

I wanted you to see what the definitions of amateur and professional are. I threw in professional employee to get an idea of what the general consensus is when it comes to viewing people and what they do as a job. I find it quite interesting that when you look at almost all the definitions for amateur and professional, money seems to be the distinguishing factor among them. There is also a time element that is included. Whether a person does something as a pastime or as a profession makes a difference as well. Yet when you go to work, no matter what occupation it might be, the employer wants to see their employee show "professionalism." A person can be called an amateur, but they are to show professionalism. Also when looking at the definition of amateur, it says that the difference between the amateur and the professional is money, but the attributes of the professional should be present in both cases. So in my thinking, should I not be called a professional, whether I am paid or not if the expectation of professionalism is present in the mindset of the employer?" It begs the question, "What is the definition of professionalism?"

Professionalism – 1. The competence or skill expected of a professional

2. The practicing of an activity, especially a sport, by professional rather than amateur players

Source (www.google.com)

Webster defines professionalism as, "the conduct, aims, or qualities that characterize or mark a profession or a professional person."

I recall in my job with The Fairmount Park Commission, any training that we were sent to, as supervisors or managers, was for the purpose of performing our jobs better. It was for the purpose of professional development, I would assume, because we were told and considered to be professionals. But according to the definitions, especially the definition of a professional employee, there are many jobs that don't fit into the description that the definition depicts. For me, there seems to be some confusion when it comes to the meaning of amateur and professional if not differentiated by money. However, maybe the definition needs to be changed to include attitude as well. A person is an amateur but needs to carry themselves as a professional, yet they are not considered to be a professional because they're not getting paid. What characteristics is a professional employee supposed to have? According to the professional employee definition, one must exhibit intellectual ability and have been to a higher education institution. Really? The definition clearly makes a distinction between what they believe a professional is to be. Most individuals would not fit into their definition.

Let's approach professionalism and amateurism from a different perspective. By doing so, we might have to change the definition. As a believer in Jesus who worked in a setting where most co-workers weren't believers, what am I supposed to be demonstrating to them? You got it – Christ-likeness. I then must ask a question when engaging the Scripture and looking at how Jesus carried Himself. Would you consider Him to be an example of what a professional is to look like? If Jesus is the "I AM," and He is able to be everything that I need Him to be, then He is the professional that I need to be emulating. When Jesus' engagement of people is examined, we are able to see that He was the ultimate professional. Isn't it interesting that we do not associate being a professional with the attribute of love? Love is the backdrop of how we should treat people. Jesus is love and, therefore, exhibits the capacity of giving what is needed to a person in any given situation. We see characteristics such as, humility, meekness, kindness, goodness, faithfulness, long-suffering, and patience being displayed by Jesus as He serves in His position (in the flesh) on earth.

As mentioned previously, Jesus is on assignment on earth. His purpose is to redeem humankind by dying on the cross for sin. He is to, over a period of 3 years, operate in ministry through the Spirit that reveals who He is at various times to those who are around

Him – that is, His being the Messiah. This is Jesus working, doing ministry and not getting paid for what He is doing. In fact, He pays for us with His dying on the cross. Think about that concept: Instead of Him being paid for doing ministry, He "pays" to do ministry with his life. Would you call that professional? Being a professional, from this perspective, is an attitude. It isn't based on receiving money. I am a professional because of how I treat people in the workplace. I am a professional because of how I carry out my responsibilities in the workplace. I am a professional because of how I react to the things that happen to me in the workplace. I am a professional because of my attitude when faced with all types of circumstances in the workplace. The love that is received from Jesus plays into all of these actions, especially those manifested toward co-workers. To be honest, I have never heard or read anything about Jesus being a professional. That doesn't mean that it has never been written about, but if it has, I have never read or heard it. What is being penned by me at this moment is illumination (enlightenment) that has been given through God's Spirit. The Scripture is full of the revelation of God Who, over time, illuminates His truths to us at various points in our lives. The Bible is so exhaustive, we will never understand or receive everything that there is to know about God through Jesus. However, it is nice to continue to see and experience more and more of who God is in our lives.

When Jesus was on the cross, He was at work. He was performing the final task that would be acceptable to the Father to free us from sin. Would you call what Jesus was doing in this moment the work of a professional? I would! He had displayed a deep concern for us as He lived out those 3 years in ministry prior to going to the cross. He loved well; He healed those who were sick and had various health issues, both mental and physical, and He displayed power that indicated that He was God. This is God working through Jesus, the God-Man, showing us how to live life as a professional, not just work as a profession. Jesus, for those 3 years, never got off course or took a detour from his job assignment. He never complained or threw a temper tantrum because He didn't get His way. He never stormed out of a room in anger. Yes, He got angry; we talked about that already. Jesus didn't gossip on someone or tell them to go to a place where it's hot. Jesus didn't back down from those who were against Him, and He never sought retribution toward His enemies. Jesus maintained a consistent attitude of moving toward people with love. Jesus was the ultimate professional, showing us how to approach work every day. As believers, we should approach work the same as Jesus did.

When we consider what the Bible shows, through Jesus, about professionalism, the definition must change. Here is how I would say it. Remember, this definition is going to be from a spiritual perspective.

Professional: a person who is of any occupation, who exhibits character and integrity and who is able to perform their job faithfully as unto the Lord, having an attitude of service toward those who work with them and to those whom they serve in the public domain – **Crawford Clark**

As you can see, I didn't mention money in the definition. So what is an amateur? They are merely those who are in learning mode. So an amateur is different from the professional in regard to their knowledge and understanding of how to implement biblical principles that apply to being a professional. Once the person has become consistent with how they perform their job, that will determine whether they are a professional or not. Does that mean we can apply another term? Absolutely! Let's add "Semi-Professional," which means that the person is anywhere between amateur and professional, on their way to achieving their status as a professional. Semi-Professional could be broad based.

Every person who has a job is able to be a professional. When a person volunteers, they are working. Does that mean that they are no longer a professional? I say not. For believers, our thinking about our job needs to be far different than those who don't know Jesus. Our professionalism that is Christ-centered can be what ministers to them. Our attitude of serving and loving can pay huge dividends, not only for the employer, but for the kingdom. I started this chapter off by talking about the house being renovated. We are able to choose who we want to do it, whether ourselves, someone who has skills or those who are licensed and skilled. Well, I experienced all of the above options when we purchased the house. My friend started working on it, but ended up not completing much of it due to his own personal issues. I then had to step in and learn how to do some things myself, while getting a professional to do some things that I was not able do. Those days were quite fun. We ended up having a nice remodeled home that was quite comfortable and warm. There was the amateur, the skilled, and the licensed skilled. When I think about this, I can definitely say that I was an amateur; I acknowledged that. Still, to this day I am an amateur when it comes to certain areas such as home renovation. However, I am a professional when it comes to what I do in ministry.

If professionalism is expected from employers, what do they mean by the term? Is one supposed to act like a professional, yet their job title doesn't reflect that? Is a person who was considered to be a professional by definition, such as a lawyer or doctor, if retired and now volunteering for an organization, not to still be considered a professional? Maybe it is time the definition be changed, or at least the subject talked about. If Jesus is truly the Ultimate Professional, as followers of Jesus, we should get our cues from Him. As believers, let's go to work every day, dressed with the proper attitude and work with a higher purpose in mind, which is to glorify God. Professionalism, from God's perspective, begins with attitude and ends with action. It doesn't matter what the definition of professional is in the dictionary, when Jesus existed before the dictionary; *He* is the definition of a professional.

Just as Jesus moved toward the work of the cross with love and focus, we are to approach whatever job we have with love and focus. Knowing that there is a higher purpose in our work and that God wants me to be a professional like His Son, let's make every effort to do just that.

Chapter 14

PEOPLE OF GRATEFULNESS AND THANKFULNESS

I FOUND IT ABSOLUTELY INCREDULOUS THAT THERE ARE SO MANY PEOPLE who live in a place where they have a access to everything, are able to buy mostly anything that they want when they want, go any place that they want to go and have the freedom to do whatever they want to do, yet many are truly ungrateful. But it isn't just being ungrateful; it is also having a heart that does not appear to be thankful. There seems to be a constant display of an attitude that indicates that they can never have enough. It is like having everything, but never being satisfied. It is quite apparent that living in the United States, which is one of the richest nations in the world creates, in some of its citizenry, a feeling that their government isn't providing enough for them even in the midst of having everything. Most of the citizenry feels that regulations from the government should be in place so that the people can have more. Isn't that what the current climate in our country is exhibiting? We are living in a culture that is never satisfied. We are living in a political climate that has become toxic and is not based on rational thinking, but is based on the appeal to the emotions of those who feel that there is an unfair disparity among us. I don't doubt that some of the sentiment being expressed is legitimate; however, the approaches that many of the current politicians have are senseless and ineffective.

When I look at not only many teenagers but many adults as well, there seems to be a huge expectation of entitlement; our culture reeks of it. This mindset has been a big part of the thinking patterns of the last few generations. In the midst of these patterns, there has been an element that has obviously been missing, that being gratefulness and thankfulness. I find that many people, in general, are just ungrateful. The ungratefulness, I believe, indicates a lack of thankfulness. This attitude of entitlement has created an environment that basically screams, "What I get, I am supposed to get and you should have no problem giving it to me." We have seen this attitude over and over again. Parents can buy their children all types of toys that they have asked for and as soon as another new one is advertised on the TV, they want it. The newest gadget must be purchased because one cannot survive without it. A new cell phone must be purchased because it is the newest and latest model, and one must have it. The latest TV has been released and it must be added to our room, even though the one in the room already works. A family must move from a smaller house into a bigger one. This even happens after the children have grown up and are out of the house. In some cases, there might be one child who may still be at home when the decision is made to move.

If we take into account how advertisements and television shape our minds, we are able to see why the majority of people feel they need all these creature comforts. It is because we are told we need them, and then we endeavor to get them, even if it means to go into debt. Most people don't think whether something is necessary or not; they just want to have it. And since our culture is one that doesn't necessarily adhere to patience when desiring something, the attitude is to get it *now*. The mindset is one that exhibits the desire for instantaneous self-gratification.

I must admit that my wife and I somewhat spoiled our children by giving them almost everything they wanted. My daughter loved Barbie dolls and would get them both on her birthday and at Christmas. What is so funny is that the clothes would always end up off the dolls and the dolls would all look the same: naked! Barbie dolls without clothes was the typical look at the time. My son, David, loved video games. We would mainly stick with sport games at the time. Of course when he got older, he deviated from the sports to other games, the ones we didn't allow him to have when he was younger. We went on vacations a few times a year traveling to all kinds of places. The kids, because of homeschooling, could sleep longer each day. They received so many things, I can't even name them all. The kids did appear to expect that this was supposed to happen – that is, being able to have everything their hearts desired. Most kids feel that way. We give and give and give, even to the point of not taking our own needs into account, and they don't even appreciate what we have done for them or have given to them. There is always this insatiable need to have more. The more they get, the more they want, and the more they expect to get even when they have received everything; all of this has helped to instill in them this sense of entitlement. What is interesting about this dynamic of entitlement over the years is that many of these kids who had everything and are adults now, don't even bother to say "thank you" when you give them something. That is also part of the problem, in general, with what has happened to individuals with this entitlement mentality. Attached to this mentality is an ungrateful attitude. This attitude has also permeated the workplace. In fact, I would venture to say that if you talk to most employers, they would tell you that the employees who are the most problematic are those with a mindset of entitlement. There is an expectation that supervisors or managers are supposed to do things for them. What kind of things? Alright, let's see! I can only tell you what the experience was for me at working with the City. Here are some of the attitudes.

- The rules are not supposed to apply to them. They should be able to do what they want when they want. For example: why can't they pick up breakfast while on their way to the work site? What is the big deal?
- So what if they come in a few minutes late? They are going by the bus schedule and they won't be leaving the yard until a half hour later anyway.
- Why can't they stop and pay a bill or grab something at the store? The place is on the route to where they are going.
- Why can't they cut out a few minutes early in order to beat the traffic?
- Why can't I they do what they just saw another employee do?
- Why can't they wear headphones while they are working? Other managers and supervisors let them do it.

The list goes on and on. There are expectations that co-workers will have - and totally feel that they should be given - special treatment because they actually came to work. Their being at work is something that should be celebrated. I, as the manager, should be happy that they came in to work and their being late should not be a problem. I should be happy that they emptied the trash can; why did they need to pick up the paper that was on the ground around the trashcan? What an attitude!

I must say that supervisors and managers can exhibit these attitudes as well. There are employees that will have a great work ethic and will go beyond what is asked of them, and their supervisors expect that is what they should be doing all the time. The manager's not expressing gratitude to that worker can cause the worker to feel that they are not being appreciated or that the supervisor feels that there's nothing special about how they approach work and that it doesn't matter; all employees are the same.

Gratefulness and thankfulness should be a quality of all people; unfortunately, it isn't the case. It is quite common to do something for a co-worker and they not even say thank you. This type of attitude most likely exists in that person's home life and in other places with other people. People who are ungrateful show ungratefulness with everybody. The entitlement mentality is worn by the person on a regular basis. There are, of course, exceptions where there is a discrimination that is being shown by a person with one particular person or group of people. For example, a co-worker doesn't say thank you or even speak to a certain person or ethnic group. I have experienced this; it does truly exist.

What does the word "grateful" mean? It means to show an appreciation of kindness, deeply appreciative of benefits received. Here is what we need to know about this definition: To be grateful is different than to be thankful even though they are often used interchangeably. So let's break it down:

Grateful –feeling or showing appreciation for something done or received

Thankful –feeling pleased and relieved

Source ("www.smartleadershiphut.com")

- So both grateful and thankful are positive feelings that are generated by an event or an action. The difference, as you probably can see, is that gratefulness is directed outwardly toward another person, while thankfulness is generated inside the person.
- Gratefulness comes about by what has happened outside of you. For example, you are grateful because someone has helped you, someone likes you, the book you received, a kiss you were given, etc. Gratefulness always needs someone else. Gratefulness cannot be generated on its own.
- Thankfulness is a feeling you can generate on your own because it is derived from the inside of a person. The outside circumstances can still be the same, but the feeling is different.

Source ("www.smartleadershiphut.com")

I am going to use an example that I personally experienced a few times to make my point. For two years in a row, I have had the opportunity of going to the country of Haiti on a Mission Trip. I had never been on a Mission Trip before until last year. One of the responsibilities that I had in the position at church as pastoral associate was missions. Through this experience, I was blessed by people we encountered in Haiti who demonstrate the attribute that we are talking about. We went there last year with a team of 8 people. This year, there was a team of 5 people. Both times, I encountered people who exhibit thankfulness with regularity. They are thankful from the inside despite their circumstances on the outside. On the outside, the feeling of thankfulness can be seen. This is due to their deep faith in a God, whom they love dearly. They express this love toward God on the outside through their singing and dancing before the Lord. They exhibit a genuine faith that is expressed outwardly in their worship. It didn't matter that, for us as observers, there was a language difference; the people there speak creole. We were able to feel the presence of God through their singing and dancing as they expressed their thankfulness, generated by Who they know on the inside. They are thankful, though they don't have much. Not having much has given them an understanding of God that most of us might not ever understand. They worship like it will be their last opportunity to do so.

Last year, the team helped to work on a house, trained leaders and worked with the kids. This year the team worked with the kids, trained leaders and others in the area of marriage and family, as well as purchased, packaged and handed out food. We also provided for some other physical needs. Because of what we did for them, they displayed gratefulness. They were appreciative for what we had done for them. They expressed their feeling of gratitude by their verbal expressions, as well as their hugs and handshakes for what was done for them by us. Gratefulness was the feeling that was generated by what was done by us. They displayed thankfulness *and* gratefulness.

We are now able to see the difference in the two meanings through these Haitian Christians. The difference between gratefulness versus thankfulness is that with thankfulness, one can experience happiness and joy and gratitude on their own without being dependent on others. I am sure that these Haitian Christians worship God the same in every service. Their expression of joy through singing and dancing comes from a deep place of thankfulness that is inside of them. It didn't take us as a team going to Haiti to generate their worship. This expression can be experienced no matter when we would have shown up there. However, when we do show up there, there will be an attitude of gratefulness by our just being there.

No matter where we find ourselves in life – whether at a job that we would consider to be awful, a job that we would consider to be a dead end, a job that we totally hate, or a job that we wanted to leave 10 or 15 years ago – there is something about that job that one can be thankful for. In the midst of loss – such as many of those who have lost everything in a tornado, hurricane or flood – the person/persons still has/have their life/lives. A person has the ability to choose how to react to their circumstances. I was reading an article online and it mentioned a man named Viktor Frankl. He was an Austrian neurologist and psychologist as well as a Holocaust Survivor.

"While being tortured in the Auschwitz concentration camp, he found that he still had the power to choose how to react to his circumstances. This gave him the power to survive. He said that between stimulus and response, there is a space in which you have the power to choose your response, for growth and freedom. Viktor Frankl also said there is no such thing as an obstacle, or a problem or a setback; there is only an opportunity to react differently than we're used to."

Source ("www.smartleadershiphut.com")

For us as believers, our attitudes should be one that consistently expresses thankfulness *and* gratefulness. If our hearts are truly changed because of the gospel, we have a heart that has the capacity to bring forth thanksgiving. Here are some Scriptures that describe how we should be on a regular basis:

> **2 Corinthians 4:15 (AMP)**15 For all [these] things are [taking place] for your sake, so that the more grace (divine favor and spiritual blessing) extends to more and more people *and* multiplies through the many, the more thanksgiving may increase [and rebound] to the glory of God.

> **Jeremiah 30:19 (AMP)**19 Out of them [city and palace] will come songs of thanksgiving and the voices of those who make merry. And I will multiply them, and they will not be few; I will also glorify them, and they will not be small.

> **Psalm 9:1 (AMP)** I WILL praise You, O Lord, with my whole heart; I will show forth (recount and tell aloud) all Your marvelous works *and* wonderful deeds!

Philippians 4:6-7 (AMP)6 Do not fret *or* have any anxiety about anything, but in every circumstance *and* in everything, by prayer and petition (definite requests), with thanksgiving, continue to make your wants known to God. 7 And God's peace [shall be yours, that tranquil state of a soul assured of its salvation through Christ, and so fearing nothing from God and being content with its earthly lot of whatever sort that is, that peace] which transcends all understanding shall garrison *and* mount guard over your hearts and minds in Christ Jesus.

Colossians 3:16 (AMP)16 Let the word [spoken by] Christ (the Messiah) have its home [in your hearts and minds] *and* dwell in you in [all its] richness, as you teach and admonish *and* train one another in all insight *and* intelligence *and* wisdom [in spiritual things, and as you sing] psalms and hymns and spiritual songs, making melody to God with [His] grace in your hearts.

Psalm 107:8-9 (AMP)8 Oh, that men would praise [and confess to] the Lord for His goodness *and* loving-kindness and His wonderful works to the children of men! 9 For He satisfies the longing soul and fills the hungry soul with good.

Psalm 95:2-3 (AMP)2 Let us come before His presence with thanksgiving; let us make a joyful noise to Him with songs of praise! 3 For the Lord is a great God, and a great King above all gods.

Psalm 100:4 (AMP)4 Enter into His gates with thanksgiving *and* a thank offering and into His courts with praise! Be thankful *and* say so to Him, bless *and* affectionately praise His name!

Psalm 106:1 (AMP)1 PRAISE THE Lord! (Hallelujah!) O give thanks to the Lord, for He is good; for His mercy *and* loving-kindness endure forever!

1 Thessalonians 5:18 (AMP)18 Thank [God] in everything [no matter what the circumstances may be, be thankful and give thanks], for this is the will of God for you [who are] in Christ Jesus [the Revealer and Mediator of that will].

What powerful Scriptures that encourage us in both attributes! We are to be thankful, as well as grateful. Can you imagine if we applied both of these qualities in the workplace? I honestly believe that God would create so many opportunities to share our faith with people, we wouldn't know what to do with ourselves! But isn't that what God wants from us in the workplace? When a follower of Jesus goes to work, he or she is working for God at the same time.

That is why it is important to understand that, when we display an attitude of gratitude as well as thankfulness in the workplace, God is using those qualities as a "sweet-smelling aroma" to attract the non-believers to us. That will create many opportunities that have been brought about by our just *being*, not talking. When we operate out of being grateful and thankful, we are able to have credibility when we talk. People will *experience* Jesus first before they hear about Jesus. God wants us to be used so that people will know what it is to be in the presence of a God that is real. How does one experience this? It is through our responses to the various issues encountered daily in the workplace that co-workers will be able to encounter God through our thankfulness and gratitude in the midst of what may be unpleasant or difficult circumstances. It is during these times that Christ can be glorified in our responses to these situations in the moment. Memorizing James 1:12 as a child paid off many times in my life, especially in the workplace. I believe that this is a verse that can have a major impact on your life:

> **James 1:12 (AMP)**12 Blessed (happy, to be envied) is the man who is patient under trial *and* stands up under temptation, for when he has stood the test *and* been approved, he will receive [the victor's] crown of life which God has promised to those who love Him.

Over the years, I have seen those who say they are believers in the workplace, demonstrate a poor witness through their lives. Some over the years, who would be vocal about being a believer, have shown some of the worst attitudes that I have ever seen. I am talking about nasty! Some were very mean and treated people very unprofessionally. Attitude is very important when you're talking about how our lives are to make an impact on people around us. The development in the areas of thankfulness and gratefulness will go a long way in winning people to the Lord. The workplace is an ideal location for our faith to be tested and proven. Many have failed, but don't need to. It is not about being perfect; it is about being an example of how one responds, in most cases, to everyday situations. When co-workers experience what would be considered not the norm, they are bewildered because of it. Let's be creatures of bewilderment. As we work, God is at work in us, which will bring about fruit, not only in this life, but also in the next. Let's be people who are "thanks-living," as well as people who are extremely grateful to be used by God in ways that we never thought possible. Talk about being grateful!

Chapter 15

LET'S ACT LIKE A TEAM

IT IS EXCITING TO WATCH THE 76ERS AS THEY ATTEMPT TO WIN THE NBA Championship. Many years have passed since we were even close to being in the playoffs. For several years the team wasn't worth watching because of the product they were putting out on the court. Pain and heartache was all to be expected from a team that didn't have very good players. Last year, however, things began to change. We not only made the playoffs, we advanced to the 2nd round where we lost to the Boston Celtics. This year, we have advanced again to the second round where we are currently playing the Toronto Raptors. Each year we are hoping that it will be the year that they are able to go all the way. This year, however, there were high expectations, especially after the team acquired several new players from trades that were made mid-season. The 76ers had been going through what they called "The Process" for several years. The "Process" allowed them to have top positions in the NBA drafts. The hope was to acquire players who were good enough to positively impact the team over the long run. There would be a gradual improvement for the team as each of the draft picks was integrated into the team. Some of the moves that were made were indeed questionable. The issue for fans was that we had to wait for this process to finally be over. It was taking a toll on us as we tried to remain patient.

To be honest, some of the trades ended up being great, while others ended up being a bust. Anyway, there are players on the team who weren't on the team earlier in the season. In essence, that meant that the team had to start over in regards to how the team functioned. Anytime there are changes with players, the chemistry of the team changes. Different players will bring with them different styles and different skills. This process for most teams will take some time. This is the kind of situation that the 76ers were involved in; a nucleus of players that were new to each other had to now begin to play together in mid-season. The new players, which I believe totaled 5, would have to learn how to play with the players who were there from the beginning of the season. This is not an easy thing to do. You can remember how it was in the classroom when a new kid would walk in the room. They had just moved into the neighborhood and now their life was starting over with a new group of kids that they didn't know. It took time for them to adjust in order to fit in, that is, if they could do so at all. When you have a team with 3 to 4 players that are superstars, it is hard to get them to play as a team because a star wants to be *the* star among stars. To have them all on the same page takes work and some time. A coach must be really good in order to have stars play well together because the element of individualism has to be considered. When players are just thinking about themselves, their attitude will not bode well in fostering an environment conducive to team play. Individualism does not help a team come together as a working unit. This is what the 76ers were facing after they made these trades.

The NBA Playoffs are currently the focal point of basketball fans in Philadelphia. After losing the first game to the Toronto Raptors, the team appeared not to be playing as a team. It was like that during the regular season. Players weren't really playing up to their potential and the team chemistry wasn't present. The five starters have only played 14 games together due to injuries. Something, however, happened in the second game. It was like a switch had been turned on and the players started playing like they should. In fact, in the first series with the Nets, the 76ers appeared to awaken from their trance after one of the Nets players pushed our star player into the crowd. One of the other players came to his aid by pushing the guy who had pushed him. This moment will possibly be the moment that woke "the beast" in the 76ers and brought them together as a team. Up until that point, the team concept could not be seen very much in their play. Should they win the Championship, that push of our player by the Nets player just may end up being the turning point.

The concept of team does not just apply to sports. We are already aware that even though one person might be a superstar on the team, togetherness, focus, and the desire to win by *all* must be present in *every* team member. It is still necessary that the team operates as a single unit, and each member of that unit must know that their part is critical to the success of the team.

In the workplace, teamwork is to be expected. Of course, the type of job being performed will determine if a team concept is necessary. The majority of jobs that exist, however, will require a team effort in order to provide excellent service or to make an excellent product. There are usually mission statements and vision statements that are provided to help the employees understand that what they do is important, and that the goal of the company should always be on their minds when performing their tasks. Companies will have these statements in locations that are visible to the employees, usually posted on the wall where the employees gather or in a packet that they give to the employee when hired.

I don't know if employees, or at least most of them, truly understand that they have a personal responsibility to do whatever they do well. Why do I bring in personal responsibility? Because if we go back in time when we were first interviewed for the job we are now doing, we told our employer why we were the right person for the job. We were trying to sell ourselves and to make the employer see that we had confidence. In the interview, we gave them this great impression and told them why we were the best person to help move their company forward or to help meet the needs of their clients. After a period of time, some begin to slack off in areas and start justifying why they don't need to work the way they originally claimed they would. In many instances, there is a drop-off of productivity as well as a change in attitude. Could it possibly be that somewhere along the line, the concept of team has been lost? Could it be that the culture has influenced people too far on the other side of center in regards to focusing on themselves? We have heard over a period of years the concept of individualism begins to come to the forefront. Should it be expected that, if individuals don't think from a perspective of full participation, that they can actually be consistent in regards to focusing on others?

What happens when a person is told all of their lives to watch out for themselves? – "Take responsibility for yourself;" "Look out for number on;" "Be skeptical of everyone;" "Never trust any-body;" "Always fight for yourself!" Isn't it quite possible that being told these things so many times will cause a person to not want to be part of a team or, if they are, they have to have walls up to become totally guarded? Should we think that, if we are reacting to people in the ways mentioned above, interaction with co-workers in the workplace will not be impacted in some way? People can go through the motions of acting like they are part of a team, but will not perform at the level of participation or contribute the way that others will. The tendency is, when in a mindset that is not team-oriented, to give very little to the team and to never have a desire to go beyond the part that one plays on the team. When this attitude becomes the norm, the team concept is really no longer present. Could this be the reason why some people don't want to be married any longer and tell their spouse they want a divorce? They have lost the team perspective or have never really had it. Could it be why people become so apathetic about their work, not desiring to do it anymore?

When I was growing up in Roxborough, I used to play little league baseball. There were several teams that made up the 21st Ward Junior Baseball League. In order to be a member of one of the teams, at least when I was growing up, you first had to go through try-outs. That meant that you had to display skills at a level that would be higher than others who were trying to make the team. Every kid that wanted to play be on the team had to go through try-outs. The teams were going to be competitive and the best team at the end of season would get a trophy. That is what competition is all about. There was no such sentiment when I played indicating that every kid gets a trophy just for playing. Once you were able to make the team, you had to learn the fundamentals that were necessary. Yes, there was your part to play at your position on the field, but there were those things that indicated that you were a team player. For example, when I played baseball, here were some team fundamentals.

- Always lookout for one another
- Don't get upset if taken out the game
- Cover the areas that are appropriate when backing up the other fielders
- Encourage each other as players
- Never criticize another player unless it is corrective in nature
- Have fun together
- Don't fight each other

The above concepts of the team, except for a few, are centered around relationship. See where this is going? Being a team has a relational component. If a person doesn't know how to handle themselves well relationally, they will have a problem in the workplace, or anywhere else where being part of a team is necessary. Have you ever noticed with people that, sometimes, they prefer to be by themselves or work by themselves? Most likely it is because they don't relate to people well. They get emotionally uncomfortable if placed in a team situation. That is why many will get jobs that don't require much interaction with people. What many don't realize is that relationship skills are still necessary and that they still have to understand how positive relationships help when part of a team.

Most people know what a team is. Sports analogies are the easiest images that depict the concept of a team. Even though we can use a married couple, that doesn't necessarily equate to a team - although it should. All I have to say is, whether you're talk about baseball, football or basketball, most individuals will immediately think "team." We will also know that each sport has a certain number of players that make up that team. How come, when it comes to our jobs, the team mindset does not come into play in our thinking immediately? Just like players on the field/court in most sports, a person has a certain position at work that they perform. Just like the players on the field/court are expected to perform, the person at work is expected to perform at their position as well. If a player doesn't perform well at their position in sports, the player might be sat down for a few games. However, if the player doesn't perform well over an extended period of time, they will be benched. If even longer, over the entire season, the possibility exists that they could end up off the team or in the minors. A person who goes to their job and is under-performing over time, could possibly lose their job. There is no set standard for all jobs with regards to job performance. There are, however, performance expectations among many workplaces, although they will vary from industry to industry and from job to job.

When looking at Jesus and what He did while on earth, He established a system whereby individuals went out in pairs. We see the disciples in the book of Acts applying this pattern after Jesus returned to His Father. The 12 Apostles were part of a team of men that Jesus assembled for the purpose of establishing the church after His return to heaven. He would walk with them for 3 years, instilling *kingdom principles* in them, teaching and showing them through His example how His kingdom was to be advanced. Jesus would then turn the ministry over to the Holy Spirit, Who would be the Person Who would empower and lead the Apostles in their call to start and lead the church. Jesus had a relationship with the Apostles as he was carrying out His work on earth and He was constantly operating in the will of the Father. Jesus was training the 12 for the purpose of establishing the church after His departure. He would not be here when the church would start, at least not physically. We also see the Holy Spirit, Who is a team member of the Godhead. His time had come to perform a different function now that Jesus was no longer physically present on earth.

The Father, Son and Holy Spirit are part of the same team, but have different assignments. Isn't that like the jobs that we go to everyday? I would say that God the Father, God the Son (Jesus), and God the Holy Spirit all do what they do well. As believers, no matter what job we have, we should want to perform at a high level. Perfection and excellence should always be the target; it was/is the target for the Godhead. If we are in Jesus and He is in us, there should be no problem with us desiring to perform our job well, but also to see what we do in the bigger picture as a team. That means I might have to adjust my thinking. Here are some thoughts in question form:

- How do I see what I do daily in light of who I am?
- How important do I understand what I do to be?
- How does what I do fit into the bigger picture of the department?
- How does what I do fit into the bigger picture of God's plan?
- Are other people impacted by what I do? If, so, how much?

- Is what I do tied into others' work and what they do?
- If so, how important is what I do to the other person that my work is tied into?
- Do I see what I do as important to me and my family?
- How is my family impacted by what I do?
- Do I view my work from a team perspective?
- As a member of the team, am I carrying the weight of my responsibility?
- Am I willing to work outside the perimeters of my job description, if asked?
- Do I consider myself important to the team?
- Am I a member of more than one team? If so,...
- Do I know what those other teams are?
- Can I identify the members on the team or teams?

Some of these questions might seem silly, but I want you to see this team concept from a broader perspective that undoubtedly involves a spiritual component. No matter what employer we work for, there are stakeholders involved. A stakeholder is a person or persons, or organization/s who are concerned about and maybe affected by what I do in my job. For example, who were the stakeholders whom I dealt with on a regular basis when it came to the former Fairmount Park Commission? Most of these stakeholders are still the same today.

- The Fairmount Park Commission Commissioners
- Friends Groups
- The Philadelphia School System
- Colleges and Universities

- Organizations who uses our facilities
- Other City Departments
- City Council Members
- Citizenry of Philadelphia
- State Representatives
- Sport Teams
- Civic Associations and Groups
- Employees
- Churches

You might be asking, what does this list have to do with my job and as being a member of a team? Earlier I said that we need to see what we do from a team concept and that our perspective needs to be wider. As one of the managers at the time for The Fairmount Park Commission, my responsibility was handling maintenance issues in the parks, as well as the trees on the city streets. When a tree falls in the street during off hours, a process would begin. A call would be received by Municipal Radio, which could come from any of our stakeholders. Because the Commission is a public service agency, that means that I work for everybody, so I would get the call. I then would call the Arborist, who would call a crew go come out to handle the tree removal. Now consider park areas that people use daily as well as those areas with these tree emergencies. Who are all the users of these parks day and night? Who are the agencies, other entities and people who have interest in the park? The trees, if left lying in the street, would have an impact on the residents of that neighborhood and the people who drive on that street. If the tree is on a main street with a great deal of traffic, there will be several groups impacted, especially if occurring during rush hour.

The part that each of my guys played in the handling of the tree emergency was key in getting it resolved. However, the process starting with the person who called the police or other entity, municipal radio, and possibly others, all played a part in getting the tree emergency resolved. All of these people are part of the stakeholders' "team," and ahe stakeholders all have a concern about that tree or any other park-related issue because it could affect them. A job in public service is like that; all the stakeholders, as well as my co-workers, are tied into a network that includes the entire city. Because calls can come from any of these stakeholders, they are all in a position of an unpaid team member.

The example above, I hope, enables you to expand your concept of team. As a believer, we work for an employer, but we are also part of Team Jesus, and Team Jesus members should do everything with excellence. This also means seeing ourselves as a member of a team that does the best they can at what they do in order to make the team look good.

If the 76ers are able to maintain their present chemistry in the remaining games, that can possibly get them to the NBA finals. Playing as a team strengthens their chances. Each player knowing their role and performing it well can translate to success on the court. Understanding that we have a role at our jobs and we are to perform it well, despite how we feel, goes a long way toward helping people to see Jesus. Our actions during periods of difficulty, and/or when circumstances are not within our control, will also communicate how much Jesus has a hold on our lives. What we do has an impact on others. Even when others are not performing at a level we think they should, that should not keep us from doing our part or deter us from glorifying God with our work.

I know it can be frustrating at times in the workplace, because of what we see others doing or not doing. However, we are only responsible for ourselves; in other words, "Let the work that I do speak for me." As a member of Team Jesus, we are guaranteed that He sees what we are doing and will reward us, possibly now *and* later. Seeing ourselves as a faithful team member can have a dramatic impact on my attitude and, undoubtedly, can bring about favor from God and man. Knowing that I am part of a team can also keep me from isolating myself and sinking into a place of lonesomeness at work, thinking that no one cares about work but me. If I know that I am part of His team, He will always give me what I need. Even in situations where the team is weak, I still can be strong. Just think of what would happen if employees operated with a team mindset, where everyone just knew what to do and, when finished with their responsibilities, stepped over and helped another person without asking. That is what I am talking about! Understanding the importance of the team and being willing to step in to help others (though it isn't your job to do it), demonstrates a concept that used to exist many years ago, but is slowly becoming obsolete. The concept of helping one another is definitely being lost. But, once again, as believers, we are able to be different. What we do will not only make a difference here on earth, but also for eternity.

(NOTE: This chapter was written before the 76ers' ultimate elimination from the 2019 Eastern Conference Finals.)

Chapter 16

WHAT ABOUT FRIENDSHIPS IN THE WORKPLACE?

GROWING UP IN ROXBOROUGH AS A CHILD IN THE 60'S AND 70'S WAS quite safe. It was like that because everybody knew each other, not just on the block or around the corner, but throughout the entire neighborhood. Everybody knew everybody because they talked to each other all the time. Neighbors would stop and hold a conversation with each other as they were on their way somewhere or just walking through the neighborhood. They thought nothing of it to stop and chat for a while; neighbors spent time with each other. They went to the neighborhood stores and would also be involved in the neighborhood events. What made the neighborhood safe was the fact that everyone would look out for each other's children and property. Everyone would also know if there were individuals in the neighborhood who did not live there. There was a closeness and a camaraderie among the neighbors. What is interesting in describing these relationships between neighbors is that the word "friend" was really never used. People did not refer to their neighbors as friends. What is amazing is that these neighborhood relationships were closer than the relationships that we see today with those who are so-called "friends" on Facebook. So many people on Facebook will actually refer to everyone who has clicked on their page as being their friend. This is obviously not possible, but many will believe it to be true.

The word "friend" didn't appear to be used as frequently then as it is now. I am not saying that I am correct with the statement that I just made; rather, I am saying this through the experience that I had growing up. If we would apply the term "friend" the way it is used today to the neighborhood in which I grew up, it can easily be said that all the neighbors were friends because of the closeness that they exhibited with each other. When we look at neighbors today as opposed to years ago, there isn't anywhere near the closeness that existed back then. Neighbors don't even know each other that well anymore. We're not even going to mention about knowing neighbors a few houses away, not to mention knowing them around the corner! Today, a person who meets another person online is considered a friend after a few chats. A person can be more of a friend in a few minutes than a neighbor can in a lifetime. Something is wrong with this way of thinking. Did I miss the change in definition of the word "friend?"

In our world today, some words have multiple meanings. Some words are used in a different way than they used to be. When I was growing up, the word "gay" meant to be joyful. Today it is used in the context of someone being a homosexual. The word "dope" years ago was used to describe drugs, as well as to describe a person who was stupid. The word "dope" today is used to mean "cool." You hear it quite often these days where a person refers to something as being "dope." The term "friend" is kicked around like a football on the field these days. If you look on Facebook, there are many people who have thousands of "friends." Most of the individuals would not have been friends years ago with just a little bit of personal contact. It appears that talking to people whom one really doesn't know very well can be considered a friend online. When I say "talking to" them, I'm not referring to a vocal conversation; I mean through messaging on Facebook. People now are able to live in a virtual world where everyone that "friends" them becomes a friend. Maybe many have forgotten that people can pretend to be someone who they really aren't and hide behind a computer screen in a very effective way. We really won't know if a person is being real unless we already know who they are personally.

I wanted to open with the example of neighbors years ago being contrasted with the world of the internet today with regards to how relationships have changed. I believe it is extremely important to truly understand the genuine meaning of words. Another example of a word that has various meanings now, not in an official way, but in a way that has skewed its meaning in the culture. That is the word "Christian." Years ago, when someone said that they were a Christian, that meant that they were a Christ-follower. Today, the word Christian has been made relative. People who go to church can think that they are Christian. Those who are baptized by water can think that they are Christian. Those who grew up in a Christian home will consider themselves Christian. Those who wear a cross or crucifix around their neck might consider themselves Christian. Many who are religious and don't belong to any church will say that they are Christian. The meaning of the word has been broadened so much that the question may have to be asked, "What do you mean when you say 'Christian'?" The word "friend" is used today in the same way as the word "Christian."

People will use the term "you are a good friend," but what do they really mean by that? How many individuals in our lives would we consider to be good friends? In many cases, people will use the word "good" to indicate someone is a close friend. When you really think about it, the definition of a good friend will vary from person to person. However, one must consider that there are traits, characteristics, and qualities that most people would agree make someone a good friend.

When we usually think about a friend, it is someone who is there for you when you need them. It is someone who, when difficulties arise, will actually be there to help. Another quality that is quite apparent in a good friend is loyalty. Other words that might describe the word "loyalty" would be allegiance, faithfulness, devotion, dependability or reliability. The person can be counted on to be there no matter what the situation or circumstance might be. Still another quality is honesty. A friend should tell us when we are wrong or tell us when we are not being honest about how things really are in our lives. We are able to see that a good friend is going to be trustworthy and supportive, and they will exhibit these qualities in good times as well as bad times.

It seems to be very obvious what makes a friend a "good friend." However, we need to realize that there are "bad friends" as well. A bad friend will make us feel uncomfortable; they will not be looking out for our best interest. They might even agree with me about everything and not have any push back. It is not good to have people just to agree with us all the time. We also need to watch out for those who, out of the blue, take an interest in us – like a person whom we just met who buys an expensive gift, or someone who is overly interested in the details of our lives, or those who conceal malicious intent under the guise of kindness or trust. The tendency with individuals who are very friendly, will be to have a desire to want to be friends with everybody. Connecting with too many people is not a sign that we are going to be friends with all of them. Having fewer friends is actually better because we need to look at quality, not quantity. We also must watch our hearts and not reveal too much too soon. Allowing others to show themselves first is important and will enable us to somewhat discern who they are. When people reveal who they are, we must believe that's who they are. Maya Angelou wrote " The first time someone shows you who they are, believe them!"

It is important that we understand what a friend really is so that we can have the proper people in our lives. Since we are in the workplace for so many hours a day over a period of years, it is highly likely that friendships will be formed among co-workers. Friendships in the workplace can become sticky if one doesn't know how to put boundaries in place and exhibit a maturity that is able to navigate the complexities of workplace relationships with co-workers. I think that it is important to understand that there are different types of friendships. Let's look at them, as well as the responsibilities that are in each. These four types of friendships were part of Bill Gothord's Institute of Youth Conflicts Seminar.

- Acquaintance

1. Be alert to each new person around you
2. Have a cheerful, friendly countenance – smile

3. Learn and remember their name
4. Greet them by name
5. Ask appropriate questions which reflect interest and acceptance
6. Be a good listener
7. Remind yourself of the interest God has for them

Source (Bill Gothard's Institute of Youth Conflict Seminar – Research in Principles of Life)

- **Casual Friendship**

1. Discover their strong points
2. Learn about the hopes and desires they have for their lives
3. Develop and ask them appropriate specific questions
4. Show interest and concern if they share problems with you
5. Be honest about yourself and acknowledge your faults to them when appropriate
6. Reflect interest and trustworthiness in being a friend
7. Talk with God about them and their needs

Source (Bill Gothard's Institute of Youth Conflict Seminar – Research in Principles of Life)

- **Close Friendship**

1. See potential achievement in their life
2. Discover and discuss the specific goals they have

3. Assume a personal responsibility for the development of their goals
4. Discern the conflicts which hinder the development of these goals
5. Be creative in designing projects which would help them achieve these goals
6. Learn how to build their interest for the projects you have developed for them
7. Be alert to Scripture which would encourage or guide them

Source (Bill Gothard's Institute of Youth Conflict Seminar – Research in Principles of Life)

• **Intimate Friendship**

1. Learn how to give comfort to them through their trials and sorrows
2. Assume personal responsibility for their reputation
3. Be sensitive to traits and attitudes which need improvement in yourself and them
4. Discern basic causes of character deficiencies
5. Build interest for correction of these deficiencies/Ask them to tell you about your faults
6. Search the Scriptures for keys to a solution
7. Be committed to faithfulness, loyalty and availability

Source (Bill Gothard's Institute of Youth Conflict Seminar – Research in Principles of Life)

When you examine the lists of characteristics above carefully, you are able to see a progression in responsibility as the level of friendship deepens. What great information to know! Understanding the different levels of friendship and the responsibilities of each can help to determine what type of friendship one desires from the people with whom one is involved on a regular basis in the workplace. Again, when considering the workplace, the first priority for us is to understand that we are there to perform a task, not to make friends. Having a friend or two in the workplace is an extra added bonus in our lives, should they occur. Performing well at our work should be the first and foremost thing on our minds. If we don't understand this point first, we can become unproductive employees.

The higher one goes in responsibility in the workplace, the more difficult the establishment of friendships becomes. The reason for this is that supervisors and subordinates have different responsibilities. One manages the other and is giving directions as well as holding them accountable for what they are to do. I mentioned in an earlier chapter that I was in management. I did not have friends at the lowest level for most of my entire career. I had one person whom I became friends with while I was their direct supervisor. In this relationship, we talked about more than just work. We belonged to the same church at the time as well. We became good friends but I was able to separate our friendship outside of work from being his supervisor at work. Because I had a maturity level that was able to understand the responsibilities that went into both, I kept the relationship in context in the workplace. There were those who accused me of favoritism, but I can assure you, that I was not doing any such thing. Being that we both were Christians, we were able to encourage each other and talk about work from a perspective that was unified. We encouraged one another not only in faith, but in work. We were able to have accountability at a level beyond work. This for me was priceless.

Later on near the end of my career I had a relationship with another employee who I already knew; we weren't really friends, but he was also a believer. When I first got to know him, he was in another district. It wasn't until many years later that I became a manger over his supervisor. I wasn't directly responsible for what he did every day. After he received a promotion, he then became part of another district, eventually being under me as a supervisor. I did the same thing with him that I did with the other supervisor whom I managed. We talked about our faith and how it applied in a work setting. What a wonderful privilege that God provided where we can touch and agree together as employees and ask God to move in the employees' lives as well as asking for wisdom to best lead the employees in accomplishing the work. There was one more relationship that, over the years, has been very precious to me. This person, I got to know pretty well when I was a park manager working in the Director's office. I became friends with them as they worked in the area of human resources. This relationship was always one in which we never worked in the same area. Because this person was in a different area of the workplace, I didn't have to be as careful around employees who had been witnessing the other relationships. Still to this day, all of these individuals are my friends. I talk to them regularly. I met them in the workplace many years ago. What a blessing they all have been!

Workplace friendships for some are off limits; that is fine for some people but not all. A person doesn't have to have friends at work. If we go by our levels of friendship, we are able to see that many of them probably would fall into the acquaintance category, with a few being in the casual category. Close and intimate levels might never be reached in the workplace due to the boundaries set by some. It is best for some to keep co-workers at a distance if they feel it necessary; however, a person must be able to exhibit friendliness even though they are not engaging others in a real personal way. I must admit, out of the 3 friendships that I had established in the workplace, there is one of them I have engaged with outside of the workplace for a number of years now. I must also say that I did have a relationship with a co-worker who was my superior that I considered to be very important to me over the years. I would put him in the friend category. He has been a great resource in many areas over the years and I have valued our relationship for many reasons. He was my superior who mentored me in the early years as a manager. I still meet up with him every now and then.

Friendships in our lives help to shape who we are. Friends provide much needed support in our lives, especially for those who have issues with family or if family is no longer around. For some employees, having fiends in the workplace might be the only friends they have.

As you can see, I am not opposed to having friends in the workplace. I don't believe that most employers are opposed to it either. I still must raise the question about friendships that are established between a supervisor and a subordinate. These type of friendships, if established, must not show favoritism. There must be a clear delineation between when friendship is present verses work relationship. When we talk about relationships, whether at work or anywhere else, I believe our guide is the Spirit of God, and He is able to show us how the relationship is to be navigated. As members of the body of Christ, our relationships should be substantive in the workplace. Jesus should be reflected in how we are doing our jobs, as well as how we conduct ourselves in all work environment relationships. That means friendships that are in the workplace should cause us to be the best at what we do, not to be a poor witness because we are doing things that cause people to think ill of us.

In a previous chapter, we had talked about Jesus and how He carried out His work. Jesus worked with the disciples who He referred to as friends. Jesus was their leader and their friend at the same time. A servant leader is able to lead as well as be friends. There is no issue with Jesus being able to do both. Why should there be an issue with us if we have the Spirit of God in our lives to aid us? Jesus refers to us as being friends with Him. When we go to work, we are taking our Friend to work. This Friend helps me to do whatever it is I need to do. I have the freedom to have in my life those that I desire to have in it. Having the right people will help in my growth. Having the wrong people will take me backwards and cause me to lose ground. We should never want to lose ground. Our focus should always be to move forward. That process of moving forward undoubtedly involves friends who will come into our lives to help us get to where God wants us to be. There might be obstacles at various points, but the Holy Spirit, through the right friends, is present to keep us moving forward.

A good friend, whether at work or from somewhere else, will be exhibiting certain qualities. The qualities that emanate from that person, can now be experienced as their friend. We do need to pay attention to how we interact in the workplace as friends. If we are on the clock and we are talking about things not pertaining to work, we are not being productive with that time. Don't get me wrong;

what you do at break times and lunch times is left up to you. That time belongs to you and you are able to share during those times. What your position is will determine how you interact as well. We just need to be mindful of the rules so that we don't get accused of being duplicitous. That would not be good, especially when people are watching our lives.

With my job in ministry, there are those with whom I work that I would consider friends. As time passes, the level of friendship may change. What could cause the relationship to change? Perhaps qualities that are in those persons may change; other interests might enter into the picture, or changes in one or both individuals or circumstances. It is important to understand that we change over time and, if we don't understand what is going on with us during those times when we are changing, we won't understand the behaviors that we might be exhibiting toward others, especially our friends. As the experiences with various individuals get deeper, the friendships are getting deeper due to the comfort level with trust, faithfulness and loyalty that is present within the relationship. Friendships are rich and powerful and necessary. With work comes difficulties, and we need to deal with them as they come. God has given us people in our lives with whom we can share our frustrations, anger, and other emotions, and it can be done without judgment. Some of those people might be found in the workplace, and that is a good thing.

Can you imagine if we are able to demonstrate Christian friendships in the workplace? Once again, God desires to use us to show what genuine friends look like, friends who genuinely love one another in a work setting. I" AM," who is how God refers to Himself, wants to show up through us. He wants to be present, through our lives – a reflection of genuine friendship in the workplace. It is another avenue by which God can transform the lives of those around us. Let's be the best friend that we can be when in the workplace.

Chapter 17

IS LIFE TO BE LIVED IN "BALANCE" OR IN "MARGIN"?

MANY YEARS AGO, SOMETIME IN THE EARLY SEVENTIES, I WAS WATCHING a Phillies baseball game on television. Cable was not in existence yet. It was opening day at Veterans Stadium and people were excited about what they were about to witness. Prior to the game, a special event had taken place and it was actually shown on TV before the game. Karl Wallenda, a circus performer and tightrope walker, was going to walk on a wire that was stretched across the top of the stadium. This was one of the pregame activities that had been planned for that year. He was going to attempt this feat without any net under him. I could not believe what I was seeing – a man walking on a wire with a long pole to balance himself. I had never seen anything like it. Karl Wallenda eventually fell to his death in September 1978 while attempting to walk on a wire in Puerto Rico. He was 73 years of age when this tragedy occurred. He has grandchildren who still perform today by walking on a wire as a group.

What captivated me was how he was keeping his balance with a balance bar. After understanding the need for him having the pole, there was no way that he could have walked across the stadium on a tightrope without it. Why do tightrope walkers carry a bar? It isn't because it is a prop or just part of the act. The pole helps the walker increase their rotational inertia, which aids in maintaining stability while walking on the narrow rope/wire. The pole adds more weight below the center of gravity of the walker, which is another essential for maintaining balance. In case you don't know what rotational inertia is, it is the measure of an object's oppositional resistance to change in its direction of rotation. We actually see this rotational inertia in our daily lives. It is easy to push open a swinging door, as its rotational inertia is low. A bicycle doesn't fall over when its moving due to the rotational inertia of the wheels. Figure skaters pull their arms in to reduce their rotational inertia in order to spin faster. By carrying a bar horizontally in their hands, the tightrope walker increases the rotational inertia which minimizes his body "rotation" around the rope. The length of the pole also plays an important role: The longer the pole, the better it is for stability. The mass is spread over the rope (weight of the walker and weight of the pole) far away from the pivot point at the feet.

From the example above, we are able to see how important balance is to a tightrope walker. Balance is the key to them being able to stay on the wire and make it across to the other side. Balance seems to be an important aspect when talking about our lives as well, at least in theory. As we discussed in an earlier chapter, people in the United States are some of the busiest people in the world. Adults employed full time report working an average of 47 hours per week, which equates to nearly 6 days per week (Source – Bureau of Labor Statistics). We have discussed how work is able to consume our lives, especially when we have a desire to reach the pentacle of achievement, which is attaining the elusive "American Dream." Attempting to reach that dream can cause our lives to be, what most would consider, out of balance. It is real easy for work to take first place for many people, and with that possibility comes a cost. The cost is the time spent in other areas of life, like family. I guess a question that can be asked at this point is whether or not real balance in our lives can really be achieved.

When I hear the term "balance," I immediately think of a person's checking account and whether the account is balanced every day. These days, that is no longer a problem now that there is overdraft protection available. When I hear the word "balance," I also think about the tires on the car. When the tires aren't properly balanced, the handling of the car becomes difficult. Additionally, when I think about the word "balance," I think about the speakers in the car and the music that comes through them. The music needs to be balanced throughout the car in order to feel the surround sound impact. Balance applies to our bodies as well. We are constantly being told by nutritionists that we should have a "balanced diet," which consists of meeting the daily requirements that our bodies need in the major categories of the food pyramid. However, most people do not have or maintain a balanced diet when it comes to eating. If balance applies to all of these areas in our lives, why should we be surprised that balance should be part of our lives when it pertains to work and family relationships. If the truth be told, I would say that most people, through their actions, indicate that work is more important than their familial relationships – remember it was just mentioned that the average worker works almost 6 days a week!

I believe that when we look at the number of hours that people work as compared to the hours spent with their family, the disparity is quite stark. I have already given to you the number of hours averaged per person in regards to work. Research indicates that the amount of time the average family gets to spend together each day is 34 minutes each day (Source – Bureau of Labor Statistics). When we consider the long work hours, lengthy commutes and exhaustion, they all play a part in why this amount of family time is so short. When families do spend time together, it's often filled with non-interactive events like the cinema, television nights or computer games. There even appears to be less time when it comes to the family communicating and sharing in the areas of life that impact them the most, such as faith, personal development and community. The amount of time spent together rises for the weekend to 1 hour 37 minutes per day. That amounts to a little more than 3 hours per weekend. Six in ten families said they struggle to get the family together as a whole with just 4 meals a week eaten together as a family. When considering time coupled with tiredness, no wonder life balance is never achievable.

When we look at balance in the examples mentioned earlier, balance equates to equilibrium. What I mean is that things have to be moved, tightened, shifted, or adjusted in order for balance to be established. For example, when I adjust the radio in the car, if I want it to be balanced, I will check and make sure that the indicator line on the screen is in the middle between the front and back speakers. I will adjust the base and treble making sure that the indicator line is in the middle. I do the same with the fade. When I see the line in the middle of all 3 of those areas, I know that the radio sound is balanced. Can we actually bring balance to our lives in this kind of way? The hours that I spend with family each day will not be or even come close to equaling the hours I spend working. So maybe we really can't attain balance in our lives. This balance that somehow should be attained really sounds like a myth that appears to be real in our thinking. We could be chasing something that really doesn't exist nor ever will exist. If we use our radio analogy as our model for balance, it is almost impossible to ever attain balance in our family life. Let's use another word that might be more relevant and could possibly bring about a different way of thinking with regards to our lives, and that word is "margin." This word does not carry the weight that I believe is attached to the term "balance." The word "margin" even sounds more apropos when thinking about our relationships.

When you purchase a notebook, you will find that the paper in the notebook has lines on it. There are also red lines on each side of the paper that are there for the purpose of keeping the writing in a confined area. There is space around the entire page, which is known as the margin. There is no official writing that goes in the margin. The margin is there and can be used if desired for whatever reason deemed necessary by the user. Another definition for margin is "the edge or border of something." It is the edge, side, perimeter or boundary. Another definition is "the degree of difference or gap." Margin is also used in regard to money being borrowed. For example, stock can be purchased "on margin" when purchased through an account in a brokerage firm.

Let's take margin and apply it to our lives, including work. For most families, between the work schedules, the school schedules, extra-curricular activities, and those things that pop up unexpectedly, it is easy to understand how the busy-ness can overwhelm any family. In order for this dynamic to change, the mindset of the family must change. Without a change in the mindset, there will not be a change in behavior. We have already come to understand that balance might never be achieved no matter how hard a person tries. What exactly in the mindset must change? It really isn't that difficult when you genuinely think about the process. The family members must determine what their priority is with the family unit. If the priority is money, then the energy is going to go toward making money and the time with each other will take a backseat. They must understand that their time with each other will be limited. That will be the cost for making money the priority. Sacrifices will be made for that purpose. Another money question that needs to be answered is, "How much money does our family need in order to feel comfortable?" What neighborhood we live in would help in our determination of how much money is needed in the family. However, if the determination is made that relationship is the priority, then adjustments can possibly be made in the workload. Maybe, overtime isn't necessary anymore because of a relocation. Maybe a second job is no longer necessary because of bills being paid off. Maybe the wife doesn't have to work outside the home any longer because, after determining the costs, it is more economical for her to stay home. Maybe the children are no longer going to private school and the money now is not needed to cover the costs of schooling. I think you see what I am saying. The hours that would normally be used for work can now be invested in family relationships. If hours aren't totally given up, maybe the hours can be decreased. Maybe consideration should be given to changing jobs, which may change the schedule that would make time available for family.

When we consider the fact that God is more concerned with our relationships than our job, there should be a change in how we see our job. We should see it the way that God does. The investment in family is priceless and it will be difficult to go back to recapture the early years if they are pasted.

Where does margin come in with regards to relationships? Margin, if you look at how it applies with money, applies to relationships in the same way. For some families, every week will be different; schedules will probably change. Flexibility will be needed with the things that occur within the week as well. You can schedule the times that you can spend together but realize that emergencies occur; people's needs will surface at times you don't expect; work issues occur that might require overtime, and other disruptions can possibly take place. Margin in the relationship will allow for these possibilities and interruptions to happen without emotions flaring up.

Something else to consider with family is prioritizing the children's activities. It isn't necessary that children be involved with 3 or 4 activities. All the activities, along with the number of children that participate in them, can involve a great deal of time. The time that is used to drive them around to their various games and activities can eat into time that could possibly be used for family time together. This time might be great for exercise or for the children having fun, but if a family is having difficulty having family time together, something that the kids like doing might have to be sacrificed in order to have something that is needed much more. In the long run, what will be more productive? A family needs to consider the priority for them to determine what to change. So, valuable time can be gained that will be more profitable to the family dynamic if the family is willing to do what is needed. When a family is putting the family in front, the adjustment will be made with employment, if necessary.

The relationship that a person has with money is ultimately what will impact a decision to make, what some might consider, drastic changes. The cost that is paid is far less for many families if they make a decision to change the family dynamic so more time is available for them to spend together. If a father is needed for his family, then he needs to do what is necessary to be present with them. By "present" I mean involvement, not just being home. I am not saying to quit working; going to work is necessary as well as purposeful. However, we are not to sacrifice family on the altar of money.

In today's world, there are creative ways to bring income into the household at home. Home businesses are a way to spend time at home with family. Going to work at any time that is convenient sounds like a wonderful thing for many. Maybe a situation like working at home would be the ticket. One should not allow fear to keep them from doing it, if there is a strong desire. One must do their homework, establish a plan and begin a journey that they have been wanting to travel. Sometimes change in career is the best thing to happen for a family. If you have taken notice of changes that are being suggested, they are centering around another word that many don't think about much in today's society; that is the word "simplify." When a family simplifies, they can create "space" for time, which then opens the opportunity for relationship investment. When you really think about all of the electronic gadgets that we have – televisions, computers, cell phones, and computer games – they have all stolen precious, valuable time from families that can never be recaptured. Relationship capital can have a major impact on the family dynamic and can literally change its entire direction.

Understanding that when the family dynamic is in the midst of change, there will be difficulties and misunderstandings. Things also will not change overnight. Balance is not the goal; quality time and development in family regarding maturity in Christ is what should take place. When a family spends time in God's presence, change will come. See why margin is really the important element in regards to work and family? Margin allows for the flexibility that is needed when things happen in the midst of a family spending intentional time together. When changes occur, which undoubtedly will happen, the margin provides space. That space permits grace to be present. When grace is present, there is the absence of judgment, anger and accusations. Margin brings about a desire to want to continue to be there for the family. It creates the desire to want to be present and to feel a deep satisfaction that comes from the environment that is being created by the margin.

The approach when establishing a strong family unit while working every day is without a doubt one that is constantly being tweaked. I am sorry that it can't be like the radio dial where things can be balanced. I would rather have it be more like the paper where there is a margin and where there is less pressure because of it. There is more freedom living by margin than balance. There is more potential for growth with margin than there is with trying to bring balance. You know, I cannot balance dishes on my finger, nor will I ever attempt to try. I see entertainers doing it and it looks so easy. It isn't easy, although they make it appear so. I am sure they had to practice and practice until they were able to do it consistently. Balance in relationships and family isn't like those plates. It may always elude us no matter how hard we try. That is why margin is the way to go. I can never reach the balance goal, and if that is what most are looking to attain, I hope that they can accomplish it someday. With margin, I will be able to move in a direction that can impact my family and bring about a way in which everybody can possibly be satisfied. Satisfaction is a word that seems to sum things up.

Karl Wallenda, unfortunately lost his life on a day that the balancing pole wasn't able to help him. We don't know exactly what went wrong that day, but we see the result – his death. When looking at trying to balance our lives with work, along with the other parts of our lives, it truly is impossible. Our lives have too many "plates" that are in the air. When margin is present and a person has committed to make changes in the structure of the family in order to provide time for the family, what results is realization. Work, for most, will ebb and flow throughout a lifetime. Margin will allow for that ebb and flow will create an environment that is conducive to growth in many areas of life when the time is used productively.

We have been talking about changing the direction of our families through margin. In order to have balance, there must be equilibrium. When looking at the busy-ness of our lives, is it even possible to establish balance with all the responsibilities that are present in one's life? I have reached a conclusion that balance is not possible and the very thought of trying to balance family life and work is virtually impossible, given our lifestyles. A family must determine the time that is necessary for them to spend together. The time spent together as a family will be different for each one. What is the same in each of the families is a mindset that is determined to make family a priority. Making time to spend with each other is the key component that needs to come first. Actually putting it into practice must come from a changed mindset. Once the decision is made to spend time together, each family unit determines how they can best accomplish their goal. Choices can be made as to how the time is divided among family members. Please keep in mind that, if there are children in the family, the husband and wife must have some together-time by themselves. Establishing consistent time to spend together as a couple is a key to overall family time working; it is crucial that a couple feed the marriage. They must see themselves as the priority that holds the family together. Within the framework of the time spent together with family, margin must be present. Remember that the white space around the edge of the paper is where the margin is located. Allowing space for things to happen in our lives helps relieve the relationships of tension and emotional roller coasters when the unexpected takes place – much like the margins on notebook paper allow for other important notations to be added. Living out of margin brings about closeness and understanding in the relationship, but attempting to live by balancing everything in one's life will lead to frustration and failure. Which world would you rather have operating in your family? It is your choice.

Chapter 18

COLLATERAL BOUNTY

WAR MOVIES ARE NOT MY FAVORITE KIND OF MOVIE. TO BE HONEST, I don't really like movies that much at all. I might watch them every now and then, but not on a regular basis. I prefer sports over a movie any day. But for those who love war movies, they will know from watching them regularly what the term "collateral damage" means, I can almost be sure that in every real life war, there has been collateral damage. Unfortunately, collateral damage is a part of war, but what exactly is it anyway? It is any death, injury, or other damage inflicted on an unintended target. In American military terminology, it is used for the incidental killing or wounding of non-combatants or damage to noncombatant property during an attack on a legitimate military target. In US Military terminology, the unintentional destruction of allied or neutral targets is called "friendly fire" (Source – Wikipedia). So we can see this means that individuals who didn't have anything to do with the fighting end up being casualties because of it.

When we look at collateral damage, the term also can be applied to real life scenarios. Just the other night, I saw on the news that someone was shooting at a person in the middle of the day on the street but missed their intended target. The bullet ended up hitting someone else as a result of their not caring or lack of concern for human life. What about a husband or wife who decides to leave a marriage? When there is a split in what is supposed to be a permanent relationship, the collateral damage can be the children. In many instances, the damage that has taken place may impact them for the rest of their lives. There are many adults who experience relationship problems today due to collateral damage from their parent's separation or break up. When someone is having major issues in their life that are totally unrelated to them but, for some crazy reason, they are taking it out on another person, it is also an example of how collateral damage affects relationships. The person now becomes collateral damage in a fight that should have been had with someone else. In some instances when one person in a relationship commits adultery, there can be collateral damage as a result. It occurs when the victim will accuse the adulterer of sleeping with everybody. When the offender is seen talking to individuals of the opposite sex, the offended person will accuse them of being with the very ones they are talking with. The ones that the offender is talking with had no involvement at all with them – i.e., hurt people hurt people. This resulting conflict is an example of collateral damage.

We can see the negative effects that collateral damage causes. This damage can also be seen in the workplace. I remember after my first stint in West Philadelphia as a manager, the Director of Operations wanted to relocate the managers. Where he placed us was totally his decision. The managers, at least the ones with seniority at the time, may have had some input, but it was still left up to the director as to where he wanted to place us. I was given the Horticulture Center, which is an Arboretum located off of Montgomery and Belmont Avenues. I would now be responsible for a greenhouse, the Arboretum and the two nature centers. After this transition, I wasn't treated very well by one of my colleagues who was managing the center prior to the change. I was a recipient of an attitude that should have had nothing to do with me. This is an example of how collateral damage can happen at work.

In an earlier chapter, we talked about transference. Transference is directly tied to the term we are discussing here. Collateral damage can impact lives forever because once the damage is done, it can't be reversed. When there is a war, the war itself opens up the possibility that collateral damage can occur. Think about what happens in relationships when we don't allow God to have control. We can easily be manipulated by the Devil, other people, and by our own thinking. Collateral damage in relationships, in the majority of cases, comes about because of selfishness. Selfishness is in us; we don't have to work at it because it is there as a result of the fall. When things don't go the way that we want them to go, selfishness can come out of hiding. Behaviors that stem from that selfishness will now be manifested in the relationships of which we are a part. As soon as another person is pulled into your behaviors and reacts to them, collateral damage is next to appear. This is what can happen in the family setting on a regular basis. The parts that appear to get injured the most are those areas that are in the soul. As we learned earlier, it is in the soul where we live our lives. When a person suffers from soul injury, the affects can be felt for years.

Now that we have a clear understanding of what collateral damage is and how it affects us, we can look at its opposing side.

We call it "collateral bounty." The definition of bounty is, "something that is given generously; generosity; yield especially of a crop; good things that are given or provided freely and in large amounts." (Source: Merriam-Webster) Bounty represents something that is positive; there is no negative connotation with the word. A bounty is a reward or something that is given. Think how that applies in regards to our lives when we let people into them, especially those who can help us with our deficiencies. Opportunities for people to use their talents and gifts, as well as themselves, will always be before us. There is another view that must be brought into focus here as well, that is the aspect that is shown through the Spirit. The people that we allow in our lives, whether at work, home, church or anywhere else, are there to help shape us and mold us and to conform us into the image of Jesus.

God uses the differences of others to cross into our space. What happens when their stuff meets us? How are we impacted by it? We can be impacted by words, actions, gifts, and the mere presence of others. There is a commercial on TV that fits what I am talking about. It is a KFC commercial. Colonel Sanders is riding his bicycle in one direction on the sidewalk holding some biscuits. Another person is on skates carrying hot cross buns from the opposite direction. (If you aren't familiar with hot cross buns, they are honey buns that have sugary stripes across the top of them.) The Colonel Sanders collides with the skater and they both fly into the air. When they go into the air, the sugary stripes from the honey buns go onto the biscuits as the Colonel lands on the ground. What is created is a new product called Cinnabon Dessert Biscuits. Something had been designed that wasn't in existence before. Aren't our lives supposed to be constantly changing, being shaped and molded and developed into what Christ wants us to be? This process happens as time passes and as God uses people in our lives. What we think sometimes might be collateral damage is actually collateral bounty. Last night I saw the Philadelphia 76ers lose a heart breaker at the buzzer –a shot that was taken with less than a second left in the 4th quarter. Joel Embiid was crying after the game; he was devastated by the loss. However, this is probably what he needed, as well as all the other young players on the team. Many times, it takes pain to cause us to see the need for us to mature in areas of our life. This loss can be the difference in how he and the other players approach the playoffs next year. What appears to be collateral damage is actually collateral bounty.

In a marriage, there are many times couples do not appreciate the differences that they have between them. Those differences are what is needed to help them grow. Our weaknesses are being covered by the others' strengths. As a team approach is implemented in their relationship's mess, what comes out is bounty. This same process happens at work. We tend to look at things from a backwards perspective. Our first inclination is to lean into what we would consider to be negative and become emotionally thrown off. It is this thinking that keeps us from moving forward in our relationship with Christ. Jesus didn't view the negative things in His life as negative. He viewed what He had to endure on earth as fulfilling the will of His Father. The love for His Father was shown through His obedience to His Father. His obedience brought about a bounty for us in Him. Consider these Scriptures and see what we have in Christ:

2 Corinthians 5:17 (AMP) 17 Therefore if any person is [ingrafted] in Christ (the Messiah) he is a new creation (a new creature altogether); the old [previous moral and spiritual condition] has passed away. Behold, the fresh *and* new has come!

1 Corinthians 6:11 (AMP) 11 And such some of you were [once]. But you were washed clean (purified by a complete atonement for sin and made free from the guilt of sin), and you were consecrated (set apart, hallowed), and you were justified [pronounced righteous, by trusting] in the name of the Lord Jesus Christ and in the [Holy] Spirit of our God.

Galatians 3:26 (AMP) 26 For in Christ Jesus you are all sons of God through faith.

Galatians 3:28 (AMP) 28 There is [now no distinction] neither Jew nor Greek, there is neither slave nor free, there is not male and female; for you are all one in Christ Jesus.

Ephesians 2:10 (AMP) 10 For we are God's [own] handiwork (His workmanship), recreated in Christ Jesus, [born anew] that we may do those good works which God predestined (planned beforehand) for us [taking paths which He prepared ahead of time], that we should walk in them [living the good life which He prearranged and made ready for us to live].

Romans 8:1 (AMP) 1 THEREFORE, [there is] now no condemnation (no adjudging guilty of wrong) for those who are in Christ Jesus, *who live [and] walk not after the dictates of the flesh, but after the dictates of the Spirit.*

Ephesians 1:7 (AMP) 7 In Him we have redemption (deliverance and salvation) through His blood, the remission (forgiveness) of our offenses (shortcomings and trespasses), in accordance with the riches *and* the generosity of His gracious favor,

Ephesians 1:3 (AMP) 3 May blessing (praise, laudation, and eulogy) be to the God and Father of our Lord Jesus Christ (the Messiah) Who has blessed us *in Christ* with every spiritual (given by the Holy Spirit) blessing in the heavenly realm!

1 John 5:11 (AMP) 11 And this is that testimony (that evidence): God gave us eternal life, and this life is in His Son.

2 Timothy 1:9 (AMP) 9 [For it is He] Who delivered *and* saved us and called us with a calling in itself holy *and* leading to holiness [to a life of consecration, a vocation of holiness]; [He did it] not because of anything of merit that we have done, but because of *and* to further His own purpose and grace (unmerited favor) which was given us in Christ Jesus before the world began [eternal ages ago].

2 Thessalonians 2:13 (AMP) 13 But we, brethren beloved by the Lord, ought *and* are obligated [as those who are in debt] to give thanks always to God for you, because God chose you from the beginning *as His firstfruits (first converts)* for salvation through the sanctifying work of the [Holy] Spirit and [your] belief in (adherence to, trust in, and reliance on) the Truth.

1 Peter 2:9 (AMP) 9 But you are a chosen race, a royal priesthood, a dedicated nation, [God's] own purchased, special people, that you may set forth the wonderful deeds *and* display the virtues and perfections of Him Who called you out of darkness into His marvelous light.

1 Corinthians 1:30 (AMP) 30 But it is from Him that you have your life in Christ Jesus, Whom God made our Wisdom from God, [revealed to us a knowledge of the divine plan of salvation previously hidden, manifesting itself as] our Righteousness [thus making us upright and putting us in right standing with God], and our Consecration [making us pure and holy], and our Redemption [providing our ransom from eternal penalty for sin].

Ephesians 1:11 (AMP) 11 In Him we also were made [God's] heritage (portion) *and* we obtained an inheritance; for we had been foreordained (chosen and appointed beforehand) in accordance with His purpose, Who works out everything in agreement with the counsel *and* design of His [own] will, And if you thought that was all, there is much more.

Look at what else we have in Christ.

Psalm 139:13-16 (AMP) We are Known 13 For You did form my inward parts; You did knit me together in my mother's womb.

14 I will confess *and* praise You *for You are fearful and wonderful and* for the awful wonder of my birth! Wonderful are Your works, and that my inner self knows right well.

15 My frame was not hidden from You when I was being formed in secret [and] intricately *and* curiously wrought [as if embroidered with various colors] in the depths of the earth [a region of darkness and mystery].

16 Your eyes saw my unformed substance, and in Your book all the days [of my life] were written before ever they took shape, when as yet there was none of them.

Genesis 1:27 (AMP) Created in God's Image
27 So God created man in His own image, in the image *and* likeness of God He created him; male and female He created them.

Philippians 4:7 (AMP) Guarded by God 7 And God's peace [shall be yours, that tranquil state of a soul assured of its salvation through Christ, and so fearing nothing from God and being content with its earthly lot of whatever sort that is, that peace] which transcends all understanding shall garrison *and* mount guard over your hearts and minds in Christ Jesus.

Colossians 3:3 (AMP) Hidden in Christ 3 For [as far as this world is concerned] you have died, and your [new, real] life is hidden with Christ in God.

Philippians 4:19 (AMP) Cared For 19 And my God will liberally supply (fill to the full) your every need according to His riches in glory in Christ Jesus.

Galatians 4:7 (AMP) An Heir 7 Therefore, you are no longer a slave (bond servant) but a son; and if a son, then [it follows that you are] an heir by the aid of God, *through Christ.*

Philippians 3:20 (AMP) A Citizen of Heaven 20 But we are citizens of the state (commonwealth, homeland) which is in heaven, and from it also we earnestly *and* patiently await [the coming of] the Lord Jesus Christ (the Messiah) [as] Savior,

1 Peter 2:9 (AMP) Chosen 9 But you are a chosen race, a royal priesthood, a dedicated nation, [God's] own purchased, special people, that you may set forth the wonderful deeds *and* display the virtues and perfections of Him Who called you out of darkness into His marvelous light.

Colossians 3:12 (AMP) Beloved 12 Clothe yourselves therefore, as God's own chosen ones (His own picked representatives), [who are] purified *and* holy and well-beloved [by God Himself, by putting on behavior marked by] tenderhearted pity *and* mercy, kind feeling, a lowly opinion of yourselves, gentle ways, [and] patience [which is tireless and long-suffering, and has the power to endure whatever comes, with good temper].

Galatians 1:10 (AMP) Free from trying to win approval from others 10 Now am I trying to win the favor of men, or of God? Do I seek to please men? If I were still seeking popularity with men, I should not be a bond servant of Christ (the Messiah).

Ephesians 1:7 (AMP) We are Forgiven 7 In Him we have redemption (deliverance and salvation) through His blood, the remission (forgiveness) of our offenses (shortcomings and trespasses), in accordance with the riches *and* the generosity of His gracious favor,

Ephesians 1:5 (AMP) Adopted 5 For He foreordained us (destined us, planned in love for us) to be adopted (revealed) as His own children through Jesus Christ, in accordance with the purpose of His will [because it pleased Him and was His kind intent]—

Ephesians 1:4 (AMP) Blameless before God 4 Even as [in His love] He chose us [actually picked us out for Himself as His own] in Christ before the foundation of the world, that we should be holy (consecrated and set apart for Him) and blameless in His sight, *even* above reproach, before Him in love.

Titus 3:4-7 (AMP) Saved by Christ 4 But when the goodness and loving-kindness of God our Savior to man [as man] appeared,

5 He saved us, not because of any works of righteousness that we had done, but because of His own pity *and* mercy, by [the] cleansing [bath] of the new birth (regeneration) and renewing of the Holy Spirit,

6 Which He poured out [so] richly upon us through Jesus Christ our Savior.

7 [And He did it in order] that we might be justified by His grace (by His favor, wholly undeserved), [that we might be acknowledged and counted as conformed to the divine will in purpose, thought, and action], and that we might become heirs of eternal life according to [our] hope.

Romans 5:8 (AMP) We were worth it 8 But God shows *and* clearly proves His [own] love for us by the fact that while we were still sinners, Christ (the Messiah, the Anointed One) died for us.

Romans 6:6 (AMP) Set Free 6 We know that our old (unrenewed) self was nailed to the cross with Him in order that [our] body [which is the instrument] of sin might be made ineffective *and* inactive for evil, that we might no longer be the slaves of sin.

Romans 3:22-24 (AMP) Justified 22 Namely, the righteousness of God which comes by believing *with* personal trust *and* confident reliance on Jesus

Christ (the Messiah). [And it is meant] for all who believe. For there is no distinction,

23 Since all have sinned and are falling short of the honor *and* glory which God bestows *and* receives.

24 [All] are justified *and* made upright *and* in right standing with God, freely *and* gratuitously by His grace (His unmerited favor and mercy), through the redemption which is [provided] in Christ Jesus,

Ephesians 2:4-8 (AMP) Dearly Loved 4 But God—so rich is He in His mercy! Because of *and* in order to satisfy the great *and* wonderful *and* intense love with which He loved us,

5 Even when we were dead (slain) by [our own] shortcomings *and* trespasses, He made us alive together in fellowship *and* in union with Christ; [He gave us the very life of Christ Himself, the same new life with which He quickened Him, for] it is by grace (His favor and mercy which you did not deserve) that you are saved (delivered from judgment and made partakers of Christ's salvation).

6 And He raised us up together with Him and made us sit down together [giving us joint seating with Him] in the heavenly sphere [by virtue of our being] in Christ Jesus (the Messiah, the Anointed One).

7 He did this that He might clearly demonstrate through the ages to come the immeasurable (limitless, surpassing) riches of His free grace (His unmerited favor) in [His] kindness *and* goodness of heart toward us in Christ Jesus.

8 For it is by free grace (God's unmerited favor) that you are saved (delivered from judgment *and* made partakers of Christ's salvation) through [your] faith. And this [salvation] is not of yourselves [of your own doing, it came not through your own striving], but it is the gift of God;

1 Corinthians 6:19 (AMP) A Dwelling Place for God 19 Do you not know that your body is the temple (the very sanctuary) of the Holy Spirit Who lives within you, Whom you have received [as a Gift] from God? You are not your own...

What a bounty that we get in Christ! We are able to be recipients of the bounty because of His obedience to the Father. Jesus was the one who was able to fulfill the Father's will. Shouldn't our desire be to fulfill the will of Jesus? We do that by allowing our lives to be a vessel for God to flow through to others. As we become more like Christ, God uses everything that enters our path as instruments of change. These things should be considered bounty that enter our lives through people. Issues in others' lives can be beneficial to us without us having to go through what they are sharing. This is bounty for us when we hear stories of others. Our faith grows because of what they have shared with us. Why? ...because we are able to see that it was God who was behind it. It was God giving us, through them, insight into who He is. This is bounty. When we consider all that various men went through –specifically David in the Old Testament and Paul in the New Testament – their lives become bounty for us.

The treasure that comes from their experiences fuels our spiritual lives and helps us to live our lives in obedience to Jesus. Whether we receive physical, emotional, psychological, social, financial, relational or spiritual help from a person, behind it is bounty that blesses our lives. This bounty that is experienced does not appear to be bounty at first, but as a person tunes into the frequency of the Spirit, they will be able to recognize it.

As believers, we are to share what God gives to us. This means we are to be agents of collateral bounty. Isn't that what discipleship really is? When you think about how, over the 2000 years since Jesus went to be with the Father and the Father sent the Holy Spirit, we have seen collateral bounty in the kingdom of God. The fruit that is being produced are new disciples of Christ that enter into the kingdom. These disciples now are able to receive the bounty from Christ that helps them to live the life of a disciple. As believers, it is our job to inflict collateral damage on the kingdom of Satan by increasing the collateral bounty of God's kingdom.

Kingdom living is a lifestyle that is experiencing bounty on a regular basis. We not only are agents of Jesus, giving out bounty; we are also recipients of bounty. A pirate and his crew, in all of the pirate movies, are seeking bounty (treasure). The treasure will make them rich. What is amazing is how the pirate, who is the leader, treats the crew. He totally disrespects them, calls them names, hits them, and makes them feel worthless. The crew allows it, while they show nothing but loyalty to the pirate. Our leader, Jesus has given us treasure that we do not have to search for. He has loved us with an everlasting love. He talks to us and lets us know He genuinely cares for us; He allows us to tell Him all of our concerns; He gives us everything that we are in need of; He has provided for us a place to stay after we leave here. Jesus *is* our bounty; what more do we need?

Our work is part of our bounty that God gives to us. Gifts, talents and abilities to do different occupations while here on earth is what was given to us, so that it is a means for us to be in a place for God to use us for His purpose. Can we actually say that our job is worth more than having Jesus? The way that we allow our work to interfere with our walk with Jesus makes it appear that we are saying that through our actions. When viewing our lives from the bigger picture, our lives as believers are filled with collateral bounty, because others are impacted by what comes into, as well as comes out of, our lives. Consider all the bounty that we have, yet we still complain. Maybe after recognizing that we truly live in bounty, we will experience a transformation in our disposition, as well as our relationships.

If our perspective is tweaked to be able to see the bounty that is right before our eyes, that should change how we view work and possibly our relationships at work. God has given us everything in our lives to enjoy. That would include what we do in the workplace. Maybe it is not really our work that is a problem; maybe it is our attitude toward it. If we see our work as part of the bounty God has given to us to be used in His bigger plan for our lives, we will be more fulfilled. Let's not allow our work to bring about collateral damage, which will produce casualties. Let's work so that our collateral bounty can bring blessing to those around us.

Chapter 19

A NEW WAY OF GOING TO WORK FROM A SPIRITUAL PERSPECTIVE

GOD HIMSELF, THROUGH JESUS, CAME DOWN TO EARTH FOR A SPECIFIC purpose. That purpose was to be salvation for us, but also to show us an example and to be an example for us to follow. Jesus is personally showing us how to deal with life and how to approach life in a pragmatic way. We just have to receive what He says and incorporate those things into our lives. I believe that we can find what we need in John Chapter 14. As we look at what Jesus was saying to His disciples in one of his last interactions with them before moving toward the cross, we can find a great deal of insight. If we put that insight into practice, it will literally transform our thinking and put us on a trajectory of knowing God intimately. It can't help but to transform actions in us that will impact our lives in the workplace.

Jesus' disciples found themselves in a bad place mentally. They had been with Jesus for 3 years and thought that things were going to be different than what they were. They found themselves being discouraged, dejected, confused. disenchanted, disturbed, disillusioned, distressed and depressed. Jesus had been telling them over the entire time, in various conversations, that He was going to die. Apparently they didn't quite get it and really didn't believe it. Jesus had told them that one of them was going to deny Him. He had told them that one of them was going to betray Him – in other words, turn against him. He had told them that they were going to desert Him. He had told them that Satan was going to be coming after them, meaning they were going to have to suffer in the future. After hearing all these negative things, why would they not feel certain emotions and be troubled by all the things that they just heard pertaining to themselves? All of these things, for both Jesus and the disciples, were occurring at work. Jesus and the disciples had been together for 3 years doing the work of ministry on behalf of the Father. What was the dynamic of what Jesus was doing? Jesus was truly being an example for us to follow from a practical standpoint: Jesus had been a recruiter by choosing the disciples that were under Him; He was operating as a trainer, training the disciples to be recruiters for the kingdom of God; Jesus was doing ministry and preparing others for the ministry, and; the disciples were receiving on-the-job training from the Master Recruiter of Heaven, Jesus. At this point in time, their job environment was being turned upside down because of what Jesus had revealed to them. They all were going to be impacted, and were feeling very emotional about what had been said to them by their Boss. They were very close to the Boss and were quite upset with how things were now panning out in the workplace.

Jesus understood that His men needed some hope. He understood that their hearts and souls were downcast. Jesus understands the things that we have to deal with in our lives both at work and on the home front. He understands how our jobs impact us emotionally. He understands how deeply some of us might be tied emotionally to people in the workplace. He understands how people can be in the workplace. He Himself had to deal with those who betrayed Him, denied Him and deserted Him, yet He still loved them and eventually gave His life for them. Because Jesus walked and lived in the flesh, He was able to identify what it was like to feel every emotion in the flesh. God truly understood where His disciples were in regards to their pain and, therefore, is able to understand where we are in our pain as well, whether it stems from work issues or from our relationships elsewhere. Let's look at this powerful chapter in the Bible:

John 14:1-13 (AMP)

**1 DO NOT let your hearts be troubled (distressed, agitated). You believe in *and* adhere to *and* trust in *and* rely on God; believe in *and* adhere to *and* trust in *and* rely also on Me.
2 In My Father's house there are many dwelling places (homes). If it were not so, I would have told you; for I am going away to prepare a place for you.
3 And when (if) I go and make ready a place for you, I will come back again and will take you to Myself, that where I am you may be also.
4 And [to the place] where I am going, you know the way.
5 Thomas said to Him, Lord, we do not**

know where You are going, so how can we
know the way?

6 Jesus said to him, I am the Way and the
Truth and the Life; no one comes to the Father
except by (through) Me.

7 If you had known Me [had learned to recognize Me], you would also have known My
Father. From now on, you know Him and have
seen Him.

8 Philip said to Him, Lord, show us the Father
[cause us to see the Father—that is all we ask];
then we shall be satisfied.

9 Jesus replied, Have I been with all of you for
so long a time, and do you not recognize *and*
know Me yet, Philip? Anyone who has seen
Me has seen the Father. How can you say then,
Show us the Father?

10 Do you not believe that I am in the Father,
and that the Father is in Me? What I am telling
you I do not say on My own authority *and* of
My own accord; but the Father Who lives continually in Me does the (*His*) works (His own
miracles, deeds of power).

11 Believe Me that I am in the Father and the
Father in Me; or else believe Me for the sake
of the [very] works themselves. [If you cannot
trust Me, at least let these works that I do in
My Father's name convince you.]

12 I assure you, most solemnly I tell you, if

anyone steadfastly believes in Me, he will himself be able to do the things that I do; and he will do even greater things than these, because I go to the Father.
13 And I will do [I Myself will grant] whatever you ask in My Name [as presenting all that I AM], so that the Father may be glorified *and* extolled in (through) the Son.

I don't know if many are able to see in the above portion of Scripture and the directness of what is taking place and what Jesus is conveying not only to the disciples but to us. The very first comment that He makes to them is to not let their hearts be troubled. Jesus knows their feelings. He knows why they feel the way they feel. He knows that they are agitated and deeply troubled in the very core of their being. They are agitated in their hearts; that is the place where they live on a regular basis. The heart is where the seat of emotions are, the deepest place where the person dwells. The heart represents the person's being. Jesus wastes no time by going to the place of need. Jesus gives them the "prescription" for their "heart condition" in the next sentence. He tells them first to trust in God. Look at this picture: Jesus Himself points to the fact that the disciples need to place their trust in God first. Jesus is referring to the Father – that is, their trust needs to be centered around the Father. The Father, who is God, can be trusted and they need to look to Him for what they need. Currently they needed some hope and strength to move forward. Jesus then says that they need to trust also in Him. Why is Jesus putting Himself in that position to be trusted by them?

Jesus was the one they had been walking with for 3 years as they worked together learning and doing the things of God and the kingdom. They had spent numerous hours together, not only working together but being together as friends. Jesus was their friend, not just their Boss: but Jesus was also God. Jesus, in the flesh, had laid aside His divinity and was walking in obedience to His Father Who was giving Him directions the entire time on earth. Jesus knows the Father and had been with the Father. He knows that the Father is able to meet their needs and to address their hurts and pains, dis-affections, and dissatisfaction. He knows the Father because He was always with the Father. He was now in the flesh and was able to share with them the understanding that he had about the Father. They had the testimony of Jesus who knows the Father well. They can trust the Father and trust Him Who was sent by the Father.

Jesus then let's them know that there are many rooms in His Father's house. How would Jesus know about rooms in a house if He had never been where the Father was? He is giving the disciples more hope by sharing with them that, when He goes back home to be with the Father, He would be preparing for them their rooms in the Father's house. The Father lives in Heaven and He knows what is there and will be going back there after leaving earth. He would come back to get them at some point in the future. The house isn't really the issue here; rather it is being in the presence of the Father. Jesus conveys not only trust, but he gives something tangible that they can look forward to in their future. They were going to be with Jesus in a mansion with the Father. Disciples of Jesus receive a room in the mansion that Jesus has prepared. Jesus is still serving by preparing the house for the disciples. Can you see how Jesus is? He is always serving, not thinking about Himself. Remember in the upper room when He washed the disciples' feet? That was one of the most gracious acts of humility that one could do for someone during that time. It is in Jesus' nature to serve. Jesus is demonstrating how to live before the Father and to bring Him glory. Jesus did it perfectly; we just have to do what He did.

Jesus then makes a statement about knowing the way, on how to get to the place where He is going (vs. 4). One of the disciples says that they didn't know the way or where He was going. This is a profound statement because the disciples had worked and walked with Jesus for 3 years. Jesus had told them things about the kingdom, had done miracles, and had spent time with them. They still didn't really understand Him completely. This is a clear picture of us; we act like we know things, but really don't. What I like about Thomas, the one who makes the comment, is that he is being honest before Jesus. We need to be honest in the same way when it comes to our work. Do we really know why we are placed there? Are we really understanding how we are supposed to act at work and how we are to treat people from a spiritual perspective? Are we seeing work through the eyes of Jesus? The disciples were with God and didn't get it. We need to be open to receive what it is that God wants to reveal to us now. Ask him specifically what He wants from you in the workplace.

Jesus answers and says to Thomas (vs. 6), "I am the way and the truth and the life, No one comes to the Father except through me." Jesus lets them know that the way to the Father is through Him. There is no other way that a person can be able to be in the presence of the Father without going through the Son. I am reminded of a story about a little boy who wanted to go into a castle. He walked up to the guard at the door and said to him "I would like to see the King" The guard told him that he could not let him in the castle because he was a commoner. The boy walked away melancholy, with his head down and his face toward the ground. As the boy was walking away from the castle sad and dejected, another boy saw him and walked over to him and asked what was wrong. He told him that he wanted to see the king but that the guard would not let him in the castle to see him. The second boy said to first boy to come with him. They walked together to the bridge of the castle, past the guard into the castle. The boy couldn't believe how this other boy was able to walk past the guard into the castle with no problem whatsoever. So the boy asked the other boy after walking a slight distance, "How were you able to just walk into the castle past the guard?" The boy told him "The king is my father." What a wonderful depiction of Jesus! The way that we are able to get into the Kingdom of God to see the Father is through the Son, Jesus. Jesus knows the Father, obeys the Father and extends to us the opportunity of experiencing the presence of the Father through Him. Jesus also lets the disciples know that He is the truth and the life. Truth is in Him and they were able to experience that truth for the entire 3 years. Jesus is reality; He is revealing the reality of God in flesh.

The disciples also experienced how Jesus brought life to people. People were changed because of His presence. Things are still the same with Jesus today, in our time; Jesus is *still* truth and life. That truth is able to live in us and to shape and change our lives for the best. God has given us the ability to live out truth in the workplace. What does that look like for you? What will living in truth cause to change for you in the workplace? How will living in truth in the workplace impact others? Where Jesus is, there is truth. That means if Jesus is in me, truth is there. If I am lying, what does that indicate? If I lie without feeling conviction, then my heart is not operating out of obedience to God. Obedience to truth enables us to live and move in truth. See how this works? God's truth has an effect on our behavior. In the presence of God, there should be the flow of truth. Then we see Jesus as life; this is God's life living in us. When we see Jesus, we are seeing the life of God being lived out through Jesus as He does the work of His Father. When we see Jesus, what are we seeing in Him? Are we seeing the tangible things that He does that reflect God? That is why He is living in flesh, to show us tangibly how we are to move and live and have our being.

Let's look at the next portion of John, Chapter 14.

John 14:15-31 (AMP)

15 If you [really] love Me, you will keep (obey) My commands.
16 And I will ask the Father, and He will give you another Comforter (Counselor, Helper, Intercessor, Advocate, Strengthener, and Standby), that He may remain with you forever—
17 The Spirit of Truth, Whom the world cannot receive (welcome, take to its heart), because it does not see Him or know *and* recognize Him. But you know *and* recognize Him, for He lives with you [constantly] and will be in you.
18 I will not leave you as orphans [comfortless, desolate, bereaved, forlorn, helpless]; I will

come [back] to you.

19 Just a little while now, and the world will
not see Me anymore, but you will see Me;
because I live, you will live also.

20 At that time [when that day comes] you will
know [for yourselves] that I am in My Father,
and you [are] in Me, and I [am] in you.

21 The person who has My commands and
keeps them is the one who [really] loves Me;
and whoever [really] loves Me will be loved by
My Father, and I [too] will love him and will
show (reveal, manifest) Myself to him. [I will
let Myself be clearly seen by him and make
Myself real to him.]

22 Judas, not Iscariot, asked Him, "Lord,
how is it that You will reveal Yourself [make
Yourself real] to us and not to the world?"

23 Jesus answered, If a person [really] loves
Me, he will keep My word [obey My teaching];
and My Father will love him, and We will come
to him and make Our home (abode, special
dwelling place) with him.

24 Anyone who does not [really] love Me does
not observe *and* obey My teaching. And the
teaching which you hear *and* heed is not Mine,
but [comes] from the Father Who sent Me.

25 I have told you these things while I am still
with you.

26 But the Comforter (Counselor, Helper,

Intercessor, Advocate, Strengthener, Standby), the Holy Spirit, Whom the Father will send in My name [in My place, to represent Me and act on My behalf], He will teach you all things. And He will cause you to recall (will remind you of, bring to your remembrance) everything I have told you.

27 Peace I leave with you; My [own] peace I now give *and* bequeath to you. Not as the world gives do I give to you. Do not let your hearts be troubled, neither let them be afraid. [Stop allowing yourselves to be agitated and disturbed; and do not permit yourselves to be fearful and intimidated and cowardly and unsettled.]

28 You heard Me tell you, I am going away and I am coming [back] to you. If you [really] loved Me, you would have been glad, because I am going to the Father; for the Father is greater *and* mightier than I am.

29 And now I have told you [this] before it occurs, so that when it does take place you may believe *and* have faith in *and* rely on Me.

30 I will not talk with you much more, for the prince (evil genius, ruler) of the world is coming. And he has no claim on Me. [He has nothing in common with Me; there is nothing in Me that belongs to him, and he has no power over Me.]

31 But [Satan is coming and] I do as the Father has commanded Me, so that the world may know (be convinced) that I love the Father and that I do only what the Father has instructed Me to do. [I act in full agreement with His orders.] Rise, let us go away from here.

Jesus, in verse 15 makes a statement that should cause all of us to think. He says in **John 14:15** "If you [really] love Me, you will keep (obey) My commands." This is the bottom line for all of us. Jesus is telling His disciples that if they love Him, they need to obey His command. Where is He getting the command from? He is getting it directly from the Father. Jesus is always obedient to His Father. Why would Jesus not be truthful and say something other than what the Father desires for us? Jesus is the mediator between us and God. Jesus is the representative that came from heaven, sent by God. Then Jesus represents us before God so that we can be united back to the Father through his death on the cross. Jesus has shown His love for us. He now asks us to show our love for Him since we have experienced His love. That love is shown through our obedience.

John 14:16 says, 16 "And I will ask the Father, and He will give you another Comforter (Counselor, Helper, Intercessor, Advocate, Strengthener, and Standby), that He may remain with you forever." Jesus must leave to go back to the Father. The disciples will miss Him because of His departure. Jesus is letting them know that the Father has made arrangements to send another Counselor. Don't miss this! Jesus has revealed some more information that is important for us to understand. He says that another Counselor is coming; that means that He was Counseling while He was here on earth. Didn't Isaiah say in Chapter 9:6 of Isaiah that one was coming who was going to be called Wonderful Counselor, Mighty God, Everlasting Father, Prince of Peace? Jesus, earlier in John 14, had revealed Himself as God. Jesus also revealed Himself as Father. Now He just shed light on Himself being Counselor by stating that another Counselor is coming. Jesus in the flesh is limited to what can be done as well as to where He can go. Jesus must leave earth, in order for the Holy Spirit to come. The Holy Spirit, who is the 3rd person of the Trinity (Godhead) will now be functioning in a capacity where everyone can have the presence of God in them at the same time. The Spirit of God will empower the disciples to be able to love God and to obey Him if they surrender to the leading of the Spirit. This Spirit is also the Spirit of truth. John 14:17 17 "The Spirit of Truth, Whom the world cannot receive (welcome, take to its heart), because it does not see Him or know *and* recognize Him. But you know *and* recognize Him, for He lives with you [constantly] and will be in you." Jesus is letting us know that we have help. The Spirit, who knows all truth like Jesus did, will be with us. Can you see the picture now? We see all of God and how He helps us through all of the persons in the Godhead. All three live in us because they work in harmony with each other. When Jesus said that He is in the Father and the Father is in Him, He is talking about essence and purpose. All of God is in them; they are all able to do the same things, they just have different assignments. In other words, each member of the Godhead has a different job to perform. We are able to see how God works as a team with Himself and how they accomplish their goals. When we consider what we do at work for our employer on earth, we still need to consider what we should be doing at work for our Employer in heaven. Our Kingdom job should have the greater impact on our earthly job, not the other way around.

These verses correlate with the verses that we were looking at earlier. Jesus had said that if they love Him, they should obey His commandment. Here we are able to see that Jesus says that if He is called "Lord, Lord" by them and they don't obey His word – meaning that they are not practicing the things they been taught – then He isn't really their Lord. When one listens to Jesus, one will become rooted and grounded in their walk with God and in their convictions. They will be like a building that is built on top of a solid foundation. A solid foundation will support the storms and the floods that will inevitably come. If the foundation is on sand, when the flood comes, the house will fall down. Just think how what Jesus says correlates to our struggles in life. Because of poor foundations, most people fall apart when trials and tribulations come. Those who are on a solid foundation, which is in Christ, they will be able to withstand those trials because of Who is standing with them. Jesus is the Rock that we build our foundation on. It is when standing on Him, we are able to survive whatever flood comes our way. Remember **Isaiah 43:2-3a (AMP)** 2 "When you pass through the waters, I will be with you, and through the rivers, they will not overwhelm you. When you walk through the fire, you will not be burned *or* scorched, nor will the flame kindle upon you. 3 For I am the Lord your God, the Holy One of Israel, your Savior." When our foundation is deep within the soil of Jesus and His Word, we will survive the flood waters.

Jesus, in verse 23 of John 14, says that He and the Father dwell in the person who loves Him, that person who is obedient to Him.

That means those who do not listen to Him must consider what they are in their lives with Jesus. Following Jesus just isn't an emotional decision or a decision that requires nothing after it is made. Jesus constantly communicates with us about showing our love to Him through implementing His word in our lives in a consistent way. Jesus promises that He and the Father will abode in us; they will come and live in us. It is their living in us that transforms our lives in such a way that people can't help but see the difference in us. This would include how our lives are reflected in the workplace. Jesus also says that He will leave us with peace. This peace is different from the peace of this world. It is the peace that comes from Jesus because of His providing forgiveness for us to get us in right position with God. The peace that we experience in Him is able to help guard our hearts. It will guard our hearts against all those things – that people do, that I do, that the enemy constantly does – in order to prevent us from glorifying Jesus with our lives. Because of the presence of the Spirit, we will have understanding that will emanate from His teaching and His reminding us of all those things that Jesus had taught here on earth. The peace that comes from Jesus, who is the Prince of Peace, is able to provide peace that is beyond our understanding. It is a peace that can only be actualized from the spirit realm through the presence of the Holy Spirit.

Work is necessary and is a part of our lives on a regular basis. God, as we were able to see, is the One who initiated work. Work for God is good, and it should be for us as well. Our work is to bring God glory and our interaction and responses in the workplace are to bring Him glory as well. It is out of obedience to Jesus that we are able to prove our love for Him and the Father. Work helps to create an environment that challenges our allegiance as well as our commitment to Christ. Each day as we step into the workplace we are afforded the opportunity of representing the kingdom of God before those who are around us. We are able to use weapons that are from the spiritual realm to help fight any battles we might encounter in the workplace. As we use our weapons and as we surrender to the God who lives in us, we will be able to be used as a vessel for God to move in the workplace and for God to work through us as we work for our earthly employer. Let's pass the test that is in front of us. When we get to be in the presence of Jesus and the Father, we want to hear Them say, "Well done, good and faithful servant!"

Chapter 20

SECULAR OR SACRED? IS THERE A MAJOR DIFFERENCE?

IT IS AMUSING WHEN YOU THINK ABOUT HOW WE SEPARATE WORK WHEN it comes to Christian and non-Christian, or even paid verses volunteer. Millions of people chose what they want to do as a profession in life from literally hundreds, even thousands, of jobs that are available for those who work. If working involves producing a product or providing a service, isn't it the same process whether that work is being done in a Christian setting or what we call, secular (non-Christian)? Throughout my entire life, I have heard what you do in life for many can be a choice between full-time Christian work (working for God) and working a regular job in the world (secular).

When looking through the pages of Scripture, we are able to see that God called and established the Levites to be the ones responsible for handling the duties at the Temple. The priests then were those who came out of a particular linage. No other tribes were permitted to do the work of the priests or those who were called to specifically handle the sacred (Work of God in the Tabernacle). What the priests did for a living was specifically handling all the worship elements that took place before God, which was an exclusive work. Their responsibility was the maintenance of the Tabernacle, and later the Temple, and the sacrifices that were offered to God in the two places of worship. The responsibility that was given to the other tribes was to help sustain them through their offerings and the sacrifices to God in the two places of worship. The sacred was the worship and those elements that centered around God. What everyone else did was regular work that pertained to providing a product or service. God had equipped the people with talents that helped them to support each other. We see Cain, the one who killed his brother Able, build a city (Gen 4:17) after committing such a horrible act. Apparently, he was given the ability to organize and to build an entire city, besides being a farmer. We are able to see in the same chapter that men made musical instruments, built tents, kept livestock, made tools out of bronze and iron. By Chapter 6 of Genesis, we see God instruct Noah to build a gigantic ship that is able to hold all the animals. That means there were those who had skills to be able to build things using carpentry. There were all kinds of jobs that helped to support the needs of individuals and groups during those times. There were those who were stone masons, those who worked with cloth, those who worked with glass and those who were able to work with metal. The talents of people were given by God to serve and produce things for themselves and others. The worship in the Tabernacle, and later the Temple, was on behalf of the people and was commanded by God for them to do.

During the early part of humankind's existence, we are able to see that the talents that were given for "regular" work and the talents given for work in the worship center were both derived from the purposes of God and both were used to bring God glory. Both were used to serve others, with a likelihood of those who did not serve as priests using the bartering method to share their goods and services between themselves. These talents and services undoubtedly emerged out of the mind of God and have now been endowed by God to do through man. There was no money, at least not at this point, for which people could exchange goods and services. As time moved on, we see that humankind and their abilities to design, create, and build became more and more sophisticated. The point that I am trying to make is conveyed by these questions: Who came up with the idea of separating work into the sacred and the secular? Is there really such a thing as secular for a believer if, as the Temple for God in their body, the sacred is present everywhere they are? The physical body of a person becomes the Temple for God to dwell in, that Temple no longer being represented by a building. God is able to then use that body, in which the Spirit dwells, to support and bring forth a message (the gospel) which is able to bring about hope both verbally and through behavior. It is through this new Temple (the believer) that the sacred evolves and provides transformation. The resources, both money and people, are needed for the purpose of getting this message (the gospel) out in verbal as well as physical expression through serving. The gospel is the good news about the finished work of Christ – that is, His dying on the cross for our sins and subsequent resurrection from the grave. We are able to be brought into right relationship with God because of what He did. When we believe in that work that Jesus did at the cross through faith, we are brought into the family of God thought the Spirit of God. The question that I have is this: "When I am involved in a workplace where I am using a talent or skill God has given me, aren't I suppose to be available to give this same message (the gospel) and to be in a continual posture with an attitude to serve?" If the answer to the question is "yes" then, for a believer, why is there a distinction as to whether what I do is sacred or secular?

There are millions of people all over the world who work every day, doing what they do and getting paid money to do it. The same people will be involved with a church where they volunteer for hours doing various things in the church. If a person is actively involved through serving in a church or Christian organization as a volunteer, it is working. I believe the church, in many instances, fails to see that people who give up their time to do various things for the local church are performing tasks that are considered work. Whether we are at a job outside of the church getting a paycheck or at church working in a capacity as a volunteer not getting a paycheck, from God's view, it is the same.

One year after I started working full-time in the workforce, in the area of my major at college, I was called into ministry by God as a preacher. For me, my work has involved both worlds. I had a career as a District Manager working for the City of Philadelphia and I served as a minister in the church in various capacities at the same time. To see the full picture, I was working full time for the city, working a part time job landscaping, going to school part-time and serving as a leader in church. School for me lasted until I was 40 years of age. You can even say school was work, too – work *you* pay to do! For me, there was no difference between what I was doing, whether in church or with the City; the common denominator was the presence of God in me in both places. God in me brings the sacred to work or any other place I find myself. Because of the presence of God in me, God is now present in the place of employment, whether it be with non-Christians or Christians. Working with believers in a church doesn't necessary mean that one is going to be expressing Christian values. There are external practices that might occur with an employer whose mission is in ministry, but that do not equate to a person being used by Jesus to impact lives. When you look at the mega churches of today, which have thousands and thousands of people and employ many people to serve as staff for these churches, they are set up like corporations. The pastor becomes a CEO, while he has a supervisory staff (deacons and ministers/elders) and support staff (all other workers) to help with making the ministry work. The only difference between many of these church structures and secular business entities is the mission. The mission of the church is supposed to be the spreading of the gospel and the making of disciples. How many of these churches exist to make disciples? Many are serving as small businesses and are not having an impact on the kingdom of God, which is why they are supposed to exist. With these church institutions being so close operationally to those that we see in the secular world, what makes them different from each other? The only thing that really impacts either is having the presence of believers who are truly genuine disciples of Christ, filled with the Spirit of God and walking in His will through their obedience.

Since I was involved in both vocations at the same time, I can honestly say that people are people everywhere. Just like I had difficult people to deal with in the workplace with the City, I had to deal with difficult people in the local church. People have nasty attitudes; some are very critical; some don't speak to you; some are needy; some try to set you up; some try to get you involved in things that you should not be involved with; and some literally can't stand you! I use to think – at least for me until I accepted reality – that being around believers full-time would be wonderful. There were many occasions which I felt I should leave my city job and go into ministry full time, but God kept me from doing that.

I remember after 15 years of working with the city, it seemed as if I was struggling with what I was doing, I felt that I wasn't doing enough for God and that I should leave my wonderful, secure City job. As I look back on it, I would call what I was experiencing, "male menopause" – you know, the mid-crisis in males. You've heard of it before, I am sure! There are all kinds of stories about how men want to be younger, so they buy a sports car or purchase something expensive or they end up committing adultery – if not physically, emotionally. I wasn't going through those kind of feelings; my issue was one of significance, feeling that I wasn't where I was supposed to be in life. I had been in school and accomplished some personal goals, but I felt I wasn't using what God had given me in the right place. It was during this time, as I mentioned earlier, when I had the chance to talk to a my good friend, Pastor B.W. Hambrick. He was pastor at the Nazarene Church in Ephrata, Pennsylvania at the time. He gave me some great insight at a time when I truly was struggling with my thoughts. He told me that God is able to use me anywhere and that my life was having an impact where I was. God was using my life to bless people at work. Full-time ministry in the setting where I was at in City government was what I was doing. Pastor Hambrick's words of wisdom helped me make it through not only that year but for the next 15 years, until I was able to retire from the city after 30 years. During those next 15 years, I gained some valuable experience in the church world as well; I was an Interim pastor twice, taught school for Southern Baptist Seminary for a year, and founded a counseling ministry. I was doing all this while working with the City of Philadelphia as a District Manager for the Fairmount Park Commission.

The things that I am sharing with you are centered around this area called work. Work – whether in church or outside of the church, whether working by yourself or with others, whether paid or volunteer – is for the purpose of becoming Christlike and for bringing glory to God. My life had been bifurcated for 30 years and now, I am able to choose what I want to (?) do, as opposed to what I need to do. The work that I longed to do years ago when I was struggling I am now doing, but in a way I never anticipated. Being able to work in several communities that range from young to old is truly something I never saw coming. Every day I have the opportunity of partnering with God in ministry. But as I think about that, nothing has really changed except for the people and the environments of which I am now a part and serve. I am still the same person who goes to work needing God to go with me, filling me with His Spirit, opening my heart to hear His voice clearly, willing to be obedient to do whatever He wants me to do, and my being willing to do it. Isn't this what I was doing when I was working for the City? It is so important to see what you do as a calling by God, whether it is in the church or outside the church. When we separate the two worlds, though the environments are different, we tend to change what God wants us to be. God wants us to "be," whether we are full time in either space. "Being" is what keeps us focused on God and He is able to use us no matter where or when.

There are people who think that being in full-time ministry is being in the sacred around people who love, and have the same purpose in mind. Please don't be fooled! In a way, being around a homogeneous group of people, in many situations, will provide a false perspective of safety. Many pastors have fallen, many people have been hurt, many people have had their lives shattered because of a negative experience that occurred in what should have been a safe setting among believers. The same things that happen outside the church can happen inside the church. On a personal note, my wife and I have experienced pain in the church setting on more than one occasion under different leaders. We know the feeling of having a leader who is over your soul exhibit behavior that you never saw coming. We know what it is to have a leader fall into the grip of adultery and then to have a mindset change while in it that is not of Christ. We know what it is to have a leader lie to your face and to treat you like you are way beneath them. We know what it is to experience toxic faith and not realize it, where manipulation is more prevalent than ministry. We know what it is not to have everyone treat you like the Bible says you ought to be treated. Church isn't a gravy train and the possibility of being hurt there, as well as outside of the Church, is the same. Do you see why that is, when you consider looking at work and separating ministry from other work as if is so different? For me, because of the experiences, I have come to see both environments as the same.

The above experiences are meant to show that people are people, even when they are people of faith. Whether around people in church or outside of the church, sin is the enemy we must constantly deal with. The enemy (Satan), according to the Scripture, is like a roaring lion seeking those whom he may devour. That means that he is on the prowl looking for those who are naive to his tactics.

He is seeking all those he can find, so that they might be deceived, including those who are in church.

Looking back, I have limited my usage when it comes to describing whether work is secular or sacred. When you look at the words, they do fit the description for the environment in which one may work. When we look at the work itself, however, there is really no difference. As stated earlier, the message is what makes the difference. We can't forget God's presence as well. When the message and the presence of God are present, great things can happen.

As believers, we have the presence of God and the message of God. Let's not keep what has been given to us hidden, but let the light of our lives be shown around those who need to see it. That means it is to be shown everywhere!

FINAL WORDS

OVER A LIFETIME, A PERSON WILL SPEND AT LEAST 73,800 HOURS IN THE
workplace. For many, this number will be much higher. When in
the workplace, relationships will undoubtedly develop. If God has
made us to be relational, relationships do not stop because we are
around people in the workplace who aren't related to us. In some
cases, relatives could work with each other, but generally, that is
not the case. There will be the existence of friction possibly occurring in some relationships that come about because of our differences and perspectives. That is normal and should be expected,
when considering the process that God uses, which is not necessarily a comfortable one. God places us in these work environments, not because He desires us to just be mechanical in what
we do, but to be light there. What is a light? A light in our context
is an example of life in Jesus. A light that shines brightly and is a
reflection of the Savior or, to put it another way, a living example
of the gospel. It doesn't matter what area our employment is in or
its location; God desires us to be a light. Being a light transcends
our earthly desire to make money. Being a light can bring about a
person's life being transformed which, in God's perspective, is the
fulfillment of His perfect will. God's perfect will is what applies

to all of us, and that is to have Him on the throne of our lives as Number One and to love people well. He wants to be in control of our lives, helping us to live life according to His plan for us. His permissive will is the freedom in which we operate in His perfect will. For example, God will allow me to work at any job, which is freedom. He wants me to live through Him while performing in whatever capacity in that job. I am to keep Him first as I perform that job; this is His perfect will. When looking at His perfect will, we need to consider our talents and our gifts when choosing a profession. Working in an area that we enjoy will have a profound impact on our attitude as well as our psyche.

We were able to see through our journey in this book that a person is impacted in many aspects of their life in the workplace. Work penetrates our being and, at times, will bring about emotions that appear to be uncontrollable. Isn't this what happens in family? One member of the family, or maybe several, will do something that will bring about the manifestation of emotions. The thing is, it doesn't matter whether at work or at home with family; our response is to be one that shows light. That is why it is so crucial to understand that there is no separation of what goes on in our hearts between the two environments. We are the common denominator in both locations. We bring what is inside of us mentally and emotionally to both locations. It then becomes a question of how those elements (mental and emotional) are managed. Our responses in the heat of turmoil will reflect what has been going on inside of us. If God has been bringing about change in the inner-most parts of us through the gospel, our response will be brought about through the Holy Spirit. If there hasn't been any connection with God and allowing Him to have those areas in our lives, our response will evolve out of our flesh.

What we need to grasp is that God desires to have control of our lives, period! He knows us better than we know ourselves and can go deep within our being in order to reveal what is in us. David said this in Psalm 139:23-24 (AMP):23"Search me [thoroughly], O God, and know my heart! Try me and know my thoughts! 24And see if there is any wicked *or* hurtful way in me, and lead me in the way everlasting."

God is the only person who can see our hearts and is able to bring out the truth that is in them. Unless we allow Him to search our hearts, we can live our lives filled with lies that have been deep rooted within us for many, many years. Most people will live their entire lives without coming into the fullness of truth about themselves. Through the leading and guidance of the Holy Spirit (Third person of the Trinity), maximizing the potential in us becomes His priority. The potential for what, you might ask? The potential for us to be Jesus to those who need to experience Him in a personal way. Jesus is a personal God and is able to deal with us on a personal level. He is able to know us in a personal way. He handles us uniquely because He is the One who designed and created us the way we are. He knows our idiosyncrasies and those funny ways we have, as well as our crazy thoughts at times. Yet, He desires to move toward us and He does that whether we are at home or at work because, He works through relationships and through the actions of people around us. If you really consider how we become like Christ, it is how we learn to respond to the actions of others toward us. That is how love is able to have dominion in our lives, when we surrender totally to God having control of our responses when people's actions toward us are unrighteous. Isn't this what we see in Jesus? Throughout the entire ordeal with the Jewish leaders trapping Him and dragging Him through the legal system unjustly and then putting Him in a position to be executed without cause, Jesus responded out of love by allowing them to do it. What they did to Him was necessary to accomplish what not only had been prophesied about Him by the Prophets, but also to accomplish the will of His Father – to satisfy the debt for sin, and to show the full extent of His love for us.

Going to work every day should not be just to make money or to earn a living. Going to work is an experience and an opportunity for God to use us and for us to see Him move. God needs to move everywhere and anywhere. That is why as believers, no matter what job we find ourselves in at the time, we should understand that we should be available for God to work through as His instrument of love. We are to be light as well as salt. We are to be the one who responds differently than others when it comes to handling adversities. We are to be the best at whatever we are doing. We are to be the encourager when everyone else is being the discourager. We are to be the one who shows love even when we are being mistreated. As followers of Jesus, we need to take it personally when God says for each of us to be a witness for Him. With God being personally involved in our lives, He desires us to be different, even if no one else is being different. This is what genuine Christianity looks like; this is what a genuine disciple of Jesus is to be.

Our work experience will bring about many opportunities that will expose who we really are. Will our co-workers know that we are the real deal or not when it comes to being a follower of Jesus? Will they be able to say, "I just experienced Jesus in action?" We are Jesus' hands and feet on earth. God has afforded us a wonderful opportunity to partner with Him in the expansion of His kingdom. If we are able to see the magnitude of how God has equipped us to do what Jesus did and to effectively engage those around us with the gospel, we will see how the workplace is an extension of where Jesus is to be present. If we just trust God and allow Him to work through and in us, just think: one day we just might see the fruit in heaven that came from our witness in the workplace. What a day of rejoicing that will be!

ABOUT THE AUTHOR

DR. CRAWFORD CLARK IS THE FOUNDER AND EXECUTIVE DIRECTOR OF
With His Love Christian Ministries located in Philadelphia, PA.
For over fifteen years, Dr. Clark and his wife Beverly, a certified
Biblical counselor, has helped couples to prepare for and to have
godly marriages. He has over twenty four years of pastoral counseling experience as well as thirty four years of ministerial expe-
rience as an ordained minister. He has served in several capacities
over the years in local churches. He is currently serving as pastoral associate in Roxborough Church, as Chaplain at Masonic
Village in Lafayette Hills, PA and as primary counselor for the Epic
Church in Philadelphia. Dr. Clark is a certified Christian Counselor
and a certified life coach. He has authored one other book entitled
"Relationships – Reflection of the Image of God" (Christian Faith
Publishing). He worked for thirty years for the City of Philadelphia,
with twenty-six of those years being in management. He resides
with his wife Beverly of thirty one years and their two children,
Danielle and David.

Email: Withhislove1@juno.com

CPSIA information can be obtained
at www.ICGtesting.com
Printed in the USA
BVHW082105200919
559041BV00001B/2/P